BLACK MAN! ARE YOU STUPID?

Sakhile Sibiya

Copyright © 2021 by Sakhile Avril Harold Sibiya

Principal Editor: Edwin Ngoni Tawengwa

Editor: Emelia Mosima

Proofread by: Dr Lizzy Peega

Cover Photography: Peter Molefe

Cover Design by: Siyabonga Hlongwane of Bonga Designs

Typesetting and Layout by: Ezekiel Matope

The scanning, uploading and distribution of this book without express permission is theft of the author's intellectual property. If you would like permission to use material from the book (other than for review purposes), please contact:

Sakhile Sibiya

c/o Dimpho Consulting

E-mail: permissions@sakhilesibiya.co.za

First Edition: June 2021

ISBN – 978-0-620-89455-5

Printed in the Republic of South Africa

BLACK MAN!

ARE YOU STUPID?

DEDICATION

This is my first book, and I am excited to dedicate it to these, special people:

- My wife, Makwena, who has been my pillar of strength and a source of inspiration throughout the 33 years that we have been married. I am what I am because of you.
- My three special children, Mandla, Nqobile, and Princess Nondumiso. You are my pride and joy.
- My late parents, Flora Elizabeth Sibiya, who I used to call Tannie Maspoener, and my strong father, Mamela Richard Sibiya, who we all called, *"Die Hard"*, you lived a good 89 years in vibrancy. Thank you both for everything you did for me to become the person I am today.

FOREWORD

by

Prince Mashele.

There are times when I get the impression that black South Africans wanted freedom to become white; - freedom from themselves. I am certain this is not what motivated our leaders to engage in a liberation struggle. However, those with eyes can see the trends in black communities today that portray an inner yearning for whiteness.

Young girls dye their hair blonde; boys hang pants on their bums, with their underwear exposed, as if they are American. The so-called *"educated"* black parents who live in the formerly white suburbs of our country deem it a mark of cultural progress to speak to their children in English. The most admired and respected among us is he who wears an Italian suit, or the woman that carries a Louis Vuitton handbag from Paris.

Even our taste buds have been transformed. We now *"love"* Western cuisine. We have become experts when it comes to French wine and Scotch whisky – more than the French and the Scots themselves. In short, we are happy not to be ourselves.

I have come to the preliminary conclusion that we as black people behave the way we do because we are bereft of three supremely important things: (1) we have no heritage and culture of ideas; (2) we have no concept of success; and (3) we have no appreciation for legacy. The first is about intellectual rootedness, the second speaks to the symbols of expression, and the third is about the immortality of mortals. The Chinese have their Confucius, Caucasians have their Socrates, and the Muslims have their Al-Farabi. Some of these thinkers lived before Christ was born. The children and grandchildren of the Chinese, Europeans and Arabs, are taught to be proud of their descent from such great men of letters. They are reminded, down the ages, that they belong to elevated nations with a rich history of the work of the mind. This is what culture means to them.

Those who have visited China, or have seen it on television, will confirm that they have seen buildings that express the uniqueness of the Chinese sense of aesthetics. The same applies to Europeans. Their cities are full of works of art that tell stories of European progress. Their technological inventions do the same. In other words, there is a phenomenon that deserves to be called a *"European concept of success."* Those who are older, and therefore wiser than I am, probably know what an *"African concept of success"* means in practical terms. My honest confession is that I do not know it.

The idea of leading one's life for one's name to be remembered long after one's death does not seem to be a defining attribute of black life. In other words, the reification of thought in the realm of fabricated things has not yet entered the consciousness of black people as a means by which man immortalises himself. The Greek philosopher, Plato died in 347 BC, and yet a copy of the book he wrote, *Republic,* is in my home library today. Through this book, Plato continues to share his ideas as to how an ideal Republic ought to be organised. Such was a life driven by the desire for immortality – what popular parlance calls *"legacy."* It appears to me that *"legacy"* is yet to become the motor that propels black life.

As I said, these are my preliminary conclusions which do not constitute an authoritative or final verdict on the life and character of the black nation. Those who have spent years investigating the question will hand down authoritative judgments. I have not done this. However, what I know for sure is that a black girl who tints her hair blonde will never be white. The same way that the black parents who speak to their children in English will never become white. No matter how much they hate themselves, they will be black until they die.

> *It appears to me that "legacy" is yet to become the motor that propels black life.*

If you forgot that you are black, the book you are reading now will remind you. It will not only make you aware of your skin colour; it will reawaken you to your being part of a black nation that is in serious trouble. After reading this book, you might feel compelled to go out and look for your lost black soul, to reclaim and love yourself, to rediscover what you should have long known: that you are fully human and that you have to demonstrate your humanity through the products of your mind and hands.

TABLE OF CONTENTS

Introduction		i
1.	For the Love of Ready-made Stew	1
2.	Cultural Stupidity	35
3.	Economic Stupidity	97
4.	*"Is Kak Maar Is Oraait"*	165
5.	Do Blacks Love Themselves?	201
6.	Black Man Set Yourself Free!	233
7.	Business Unusual	253
8.	Wealth Redistribution	265
9.	Yes, We Can!	293
In Reflection		301
Acknowledgements		307

INTRODUCTION

I grew up with a curious mind. At most, I questioned the status quo of Black people. I asked many *"whys"* and *"why nots"* at a young age. At times I thought it was my juvenile mind at work, tormented by inexperience and immaturity. But I just couldn't stop myself from questioning the state of affairs to which I was exposed.

As I observed the iron fist and heavy-handed approach of the apartheid regime, I feared that my questions would land me in prison. I decided to keep the questions all to myself.

I remember how every single year, without fail, my father would be visited by vicious-looking and cruel White policemen who would interrogate him about his political involvements. These visits became more incessant and grew brutal when my father became deeply involved with the labour unions. It was as if he was a criminal and a troublemaker and had to be kept under their radar. These intimidating circumstances cemented my resolution to keep all my troubling questions to myself.

As I grew older, I could no longer avoid all these unanswered questions caged in my mind since my childhood. I chose to confront them head-on and deal with them fearlessly and ruthlessly. Now, having lived more than five decades, I purposed to engage my fellow Black people on the anomalies that plague us as a race in general and as Black South Africans in particular – *rona bana ba thari entsho – thina iSizwe esimpisholo.*

Uncomfortable Conversations with Myself

This book is the outcome of the many conversations I have had with God, self and fellow Black people from all walks of life and nationalities. Here are some of the many uncomfortable questions this book seeks to confront:

- *Why is it that Black people struggle with self-love, self-acceptance and self-appreciation?*

- *Why do Black people struggle to embrace and celebrate their cultures, languages and heritage?*
- *Why do Black people tend to idolise Whites and almost everything associated with them?*
- *Why do Black people exert themselves towards improving whatever is white while abandoning whatever is black and allowing anything that has to do with being black to deteriorate?*
- *Why have Black people adopted the White man's perspective as the standard to determine good or bad, acceptable or unacceptable, beautiful or ugly, right or wrong, excellent or average, fashionable or otherwise?*
- *Why do Black people serve all other races while none of those races serve them?*
- *Why is it that Africa is the wealthiest continent on earth in which Africans remain the poorest?*
- *Why do Black people aspire towards whiteness and detest blackness?*
- *Why do Black people view the English language as a measure of intelligence and*

> *sophistication, while other Whites, for example, the Germans and Italians, care nothing for it?*
> - *Why do Black people in South Africa enjoy the blessing of being the majority but look up to White people to feed, clothe and employ them?*
> - *Why do Black people allow White people to remain the dominant race in the mainstream economy?*
> - *And most importantly, what can the Black nation do about this sad status quo?*

Not for the Faint-Hearted

Suffice to say, this book is not a read for the faint-hearted Black man. It requires a fair amount of courage to confront this elephant in the room that nobody dares to talk about. It requires boldness to talk about these sacred cows that we shy away from for fear of political incorrectness and negative public perceptions. This conversation requires guts and shameless audacity. Because, more often than not, talking about the things that will lead to the emancipation of Black people is branded racist or hate speech.

While this book aims to be brutal, confrontational and provocative, it does not constitute hate speech in any way, shape or form. Neither does it fit into the category of racist sentiments and rhetoric. I desire to ignite the long-overdue robust debates and discussions amongst Black people at all levels. This book is a wake-up call to Black people in my nation and around the world. I seek to challenge your mindsets and behaviours; and ultimately, change the narrative of our race. I envisage Black people talking about the issues raised herein wherever they converge – at universities, colleges, churches, pubs, taverns, funerals, stokvels or socials. The message of this book must resound on busses, radio, TV, social media and in taxis.

I hope some of you will be so offended that you will be challenged to respond with the same indignant passion with which this book was written. This book does not spare any punches at all; it tells it like it is. I am completely sold out to the message of this book regardless of whatever controversy it may spark or negative connotations it may evoke. That is the steep price I am willing to pay for the liberation of the black mind from the mental oppression that has become synonymous with our race. I will not compromise! *Asijiki!* So long as this book achieves the impact it was designed for, I will be more than satisfied. So, go ahead! You can agree or disagree with me, in part or completely, as long as we can start this long-overdue dialogue.

> *I desire to ignite the long-overdue robust debates and discussions amongst Black people at all levels. This book is a wake-up call to Black people in my nation and around the world. I seek to challenge your mindsets and behaviours; and ultimately, change the narrative of our race.*

I Crave Your Indulgence

In this book, I take some hard jabs at Black people. Mercilessly, I confront the folly we continually display without relenting. I unapologetically call out our collective stupidity without fear or prejudice. Not because I have all the answers, but because we cannot hold candid and objective conversations without context. Much of what I state in this book are not opinions. They are but facts.

Facts that stare at us without blinking. Go ahead and challenge me. But challenge me with facts. Allow your emotions to lie low for now.

In this discourse, your current mental status quo as a Black person is vigorously rattled and shaken. If I enrage you, let your indignation push you to dig for facts so our conversation becomes meaty, fruitful and effective. We could then pull ourselves out of the mess in which we find ourselves. It does not matter how rough the ride gets; we must stay the course.

> *I hope some of you will be so offended that you will be challenged to respond with the same indignant passion with which this book was written.*

My Black brothers and sisters, let us have this conversation. Let us talk. Let us engage in a dialogue as a people of common ancestry, as we share our diverse perspectives on issues that matter to the Black nation. Let us create grassroots and social media communities that engage in these concerns. Furthermore, let us dig deep to find the answers to the myriad complexities that frustrates our progress. Let us have an *indaba* regarding our future. You may not agree with my perspectives, but we can agree that we need a dramatic change to the economic and cultural trajectory of our race. Therefore, we must hold objective dialogues on these issues. These conversations must continue till they culminate into actionable strategies that will lead to a radical and revolutionary recovery process for our race.

I call on those who want to create a better South Africa and world for future generations of Black children.

I call upon those who want to see our communities improve into efficiently run and well-maintained symbols of black pride, dignity and excellence. Communities where:

- *Our race and its diverse cultures are honoured and celebrated.*
- *Our languages are proudly spoken.*
- *Our people live in peace and harmony.*
- *Our people circulate money amongst themselves.*
- *Our institutions deliver exceptional service to our people – from our schools to our*

> *hospitals, businesses, government departments and others.*
> - *Our people are producers and innovators, not mere consumers and spectators.*
> - *Our people are without generational debt.*

> ***I call upon those who want to see our communities improve into efficiently run and well-maintained symbols of black pride, dignity and excellence.***

Our Generational Debt

As an act of honour and gratitude for the great sacrifices made for us by the generations of our fathers, we must address the anomalies that exist amongst us as a race and the barriers that frustrate our progress. We must do this for future generations. Our generation must one day account for its history and legacy. We must explain ourselves to posterity and account for our contribution to the cause and agenda of the Black man. The generations of Kwame Nkrumah, Oliver Tambo, Stephen Bantu Biko, Nelson Mandela, Thomas Sankara, Solomon Mahlangu, Winnie

Mandela, Samora Machel, Julius Nyerere, Robert Mugabe and Chris Hani can boldly stand and say, *"we achieved political freedom for our people"*. What about us? What can we show as our efforts to further the cause of our people? Sadly, the only thing we can show is the betrayal of our race, heritage and future generations.

> *As an act of honour and gratitude for the great sacrifices made for us by the generations of our fathers, we must address the anomalies that exist amongst us as a race and the barriers that frustrate our progress.*

The Clarion Call

This book is a clarion call to those who want to make their lives count for a cause that is greater than themselves.

- *A call to get together and have brutal, honest and fruitful conversations about ourselves.*

- *A call to take upon ourselves the responsibility to redeem the future of our race.*
- *A call to rise and shake off the bonds of mental slavery.*
- *A call to embrace and celebrate our blackness with pride, dignity and honour.*
- *A call to return to our roots as the people of ubuntu.*
- *A call to self-appreciation, self-acceptance and self-love.*
- *A call to put our political, religious, cultural, tribal, national, social, ideological and economic differences aside for a greater cause.*

In this book, I expose our attitudes as Black people towards Whites and vice versa; and this I do in the strongest possible terms, especially when referring to the white Afrikaner supremacists and white monopoly capitalists. Many will be quick to label me mad, angry and bitter. A black racist is what you might be tempted to label me. However, I am not racist, I am a Christian leader. I am called to love my neighbour, to love the one who does not look or think like me, and to even love the one I share a painful past with. I am not afraid to be perceived as racist. I will not ignore my day-to-day reality. *Askies!* I am sorry! It will not happen!

The objective of this book is not to agree with everyone or find acceptance. My objective is to get every Black person talking about the serious issues and matters that need our immediate and undivided attention as a generation. In this mission, I commit myself to call a spade a spade. I will avoid greying around black and white issues. I will not grey around the general and predominant attitudes of Blacks towards themselves, Whites towards Blacks, and those of Blacks towards Whites. I scream and shout on matters that should be on the agenda of this discourse, such as our spending patterns and day-to-day choices, in the hope that you will heed the clarion call for us to come and reason together.

Come, Let Us Reason Together

The black race in South Africa is diverse; drawn from many tribes, cultures, social and economic classes, and ethnic groups. But we are still one race and one people who can trace themselves back to common ancestry. We are all sons of the African soil. We share a common pain and reality because we all are black brothers. We have a level ground upon which we can forge common interest on matters of our concern.

> *I am called to love my neighbour, to love the one who does not look or think like me, and to even love the one I share a painful past with.*

After All is Said and Done

Once we have mustered the much-needed courage and boldness to confront these matters, we can proceed to the point of rediscovering the beauty, majesty, royalty and power of our blackness. Surely, you have heard that *"black is beautiful"*, and just so you know, I subscribe to this notion wholeheartedly. I not only believe that black is beautiful; I am convinced that black is powerful! It is my heartfelt prayer and passionate desire that one day we will see the power and beauty of our blackness unleashed on our communities once again, beginning as a flickering flame and continuing as a veld fire burning for generations to come.

You are invited, my brethren. I invite you, my dear reader. Join me on this journey to discover the answer to the question, are you free or *dom*?

Before we proceed, allow me to state the following disclaimers.

First Disclaimer

This book is the result of my reflections. As such, I am the first one in the line of fire. The stupidity I point out is the stupidity I have, in many cases, found in myself. I am just as guilty as the next Black person, and I am working daily to improve and love myself and my race more.

Second Disclaimer

There are always exceptions in life. Not all Blacks are self-hating; not all Whites are racist. I address the general trends and norms which no one can deny.

Third Disclaimer

Even though I pastor a Pentecostal/Charismatic Church, I would like it to be known that this book is not exclusively written for the Christian community. It is written for the African community regardless of their religious persuasions. So, to my *"holier than thous"*, please do not pull a Bible verse and go all spiritual on me when you come across words and nuances that are not Christian. ***Uzoba* strong!** You will be strong!

Now let us strap on our safety belts as the ride will be rough.

> *It is my heartfelt prayer and passionate desire that one day we will see the power and beauty of our blackness unleashed on our communities once again, beginning as a flickering flame and continuing as a veld fire burning for generations to come.*

1

FOR THE LOVE OF READY-MADE STEW

"Black power simply means: Look at me, I'm here. I have dignity. I have pride. I have roots. I insist, I demand that I participate in those decisions that affect my life and the lives of my children. It means that I am somebody."

Whitney M. Young

Allow me to relay a story about two brothers who lived during the ancient times of the Bible. Their names were Esau and Jacob. Both were sons of a man called Isaac. Esau was the elder, Jacob was the younger. Esau was a skilful hunter, good at exploring the forests and hunting game. As the firstborn son, Esau was the destined heir to his father's inheritance and wealth. It was his birthright and privilege according to their culture. Jacob, on the other hand, was an introvert who dwelt around the community and did not like wandering too far away from home. Whenever Esau went out to hunt, he would return home with game and prepare a scrumptious feast for the family. He did this so well for many years; his father grew fond of his meaty stews.

One Fateful Day

On one hot day, Esau had gone out hunting as it was his regular practice, only that this time he came back empty-handed and frustrated. He had been out all day and was hungry. When he entered the house, he coincidentally found Jacob preparing a stew with an inviting aroma that filled the entire house. Starved and exhausted, Esau asked his younger brother, Jacob, to dish up some of this delicious stew for him so that he could eat and satiate his famished body.

"Quick, let me have some of that red stew! I'm famished!" he said.

"First sell me your birthright," Jacob replied.

This response is strange and unexpected. I mean, what is a plate of stew between two brothers that it would warrant a destiny defining negotiation? Can't you give your hungry brother a plate of stew seeing that he is hungry and exhausted without bringing up firstborn rights and privileges? Aren't brothers supposed to be there for one another in times of hunger? What happened to being your brother's keeper?

Clearly, Jacob did not care about being brotherly. He had intentions that only he knew, so he stuck to his guns.

"Look, I am about to die," Esau said as he expressed his desperation. *"What good is a birthright to me?"*, he added.

The Oath that Changed it All

After seeing that Esau was game, Jacob, who was a crafty, calculative and cunning person, swiftly went in for the kill as a shrewd serpent would.

"Swear to me first", Jacob said to his brother.

In that very moment, without thinking it through and without considering the grave consequences of his actions, Esau made an oath to his younger brother and sold his priceless birthright to him in exchange for a mere plate of ready-made stew.

Delighted by his conquest, Jacob quickly sealed the deal. He dished out bread and some lentil stew for Esau, who ate and drank to his satisfaction before getting up and leaving the house. That way, Esau gave away his birthright for a plate of ready-made stew. Sadly, he did not realise the irreversible generational consequences of his actions. To him, it was all a worthless conversation which got him that plate of ready-made stew that his tired and famished body had been desperately craving. After all, what good is a birthright when you are about to die, and you desperately need to eat? Who eats a birthright? You might as well sell it to the lowest bidder, right?

Let us interrogate this a little further to see if the birthright he sold for a plate of ready-made stew was really of no value at all.

> *After all, what good is a birthright when you are about to die, and you desperately need to eat? Who eats a birthright? You might as well sell it to the lowest bidder, right?*

Tricked Again

Following that fateful day, many years would pass; life went on as if nothing had been exchanged between Jacob and Esau until some unfortunate events began to take place in their household. Their father, Isaac, was now advanced in age. He had become blind and frail. Feeling that his death was imminent, he called his firstborn Esau and gave him instructions to go out and hunt some good game, prepare a meal for him to eat and be satisfied; and thereafter, declare and release his *"rightful"* blessings to him.

Excited and raring to receive the birthright blessings, Esau went out to hunt the best game he could find. While he was out, his scheming brother, Jacob, and their mother, Rebekah, moved swiftly to prepare the stew that Isaac loved so much. And Jacob was able to feed his father before Esau's return. When Isaac had eaten and was satisfied with the meal that Jacob had served him, he called for Esau so that he could lay his hands on him to release the birthright blessings befitting the firstborn son. Instead of Esau stepping up, Jacob cunningly appeared before his blind father to receive the birthright blessings.

"Is this really you, my son Esau, that I am touching?" the father asked upon touching Jacob's hands. Jacob had covered his hands with a goat's skin to deceive his father, for Esau was a hairy man.

"Yes father, it is I, Esau", Jacob replied rather nervously.

Convinced that Jacob was Esau, Isaac proceeded to release Esau's entire birthright blessing upon Jacob, who was the wrongful recipient.

Isaac laid his hand upon Jacob and assertively declared: *"May God give you heaven's dew and the earth's richness and an abundance of grain and new wine. May nations serve you and people bow down to you. Be lord over your brothers and may the sons of your mother bow down to you. May those who curse you be cursed, and those who bless you be blessed."*

Not long after Isaac had unknowingly released Esau's blessings upon Jacob, Esau came in from his successful hunting trip. Excited and expectant, he went straight into the kitchen to prepare his father's favourite stew. He could not wait to receive "his blessings" as the firstborn son. Little did he know that Jacob had already been dismissed from their father's presence laden with all the blessings and affirmations that Isaac had desired to bestow upon him. Unfortunately for Esau, he had already lost the blessings of the firstborn son to Jacob in the same way he had lost the birthright to him many years earlier.

Esau's Regret

When Esau finally presented himself before his blind father, he was taken aback by his father's response.

"Who are you?" his father asked him.

"I am your son," he answered.

"Esau, your firstborn."

Isaac trembled violently and said, "Who was it then that hunted game and brought it to me to eat, just before you came in?"

"I have blessed him – and indeed he will be blessed!"

When Esau heard his father's words, he burst out with a loud and bitter cry and said to his father, "Bless me too, my father!"

But his father said, "Your brother came and deceitfully took your blessings."

Esau said, "Isn't he rightly named Jacob? This is the second time he has taken advantage of me – he took my birthright and now he has taken my blessings!"

Exasperated, Esau went on to ask his father, "Haven't you reserved another blessing for me? "

Isaac answered: *"I have made him lord over you and have made all his relatives his servants, and I have sustained him with grain and new wine."*

"So, what can I possibly do for you, my son?" Isaac asked his firstborn son, Esau.

Then Esau wept aloud.

"Do you have only one blessing, my father? Bless me too, my father!"

His father Isaac answered him: *"Your dwelling will be far away from the earth's riches; away from the dew of heaven above. You will live by the sword, and you will serve your brother. But when you grow restless, you will throw his yoke from off your neck."*

Esau's Note to Self

From that day forward, Esau held a grudge against his brother Jacob because of the blessings their father had conferred upon him.

He said to himself, *"The days of mourning for my father's death are near; after which I will kill my brother Jacob."*

The wrong brother shrewdly obtained a birthright and subsequently the rich blessings that were reserved for his elder brother. The rightful brother, who was supposed to be the heir, destined to inherit all those blessings, was condemned to struggle and servanthood. In the birthright that Esau lost, was his destiny, wealth, blessings and inheritance, as the firstborn son. He unknowingly and foolishly sold all these valuable birthright opportunities for the convenience of a mere plate of ready-made stew.

> *You will live by the sword, and you will serve your brother. But when you grow restless, you will throw his yoke from off your neck."*

Esau's Stupidity

Esau was a skilled cook who could have endured hunger and discomfort for a while and cooked his own meal. He could have addressed his problem of hunger in less than an hour if he wanted to. He did not need to foolishly swap his birthright for a mere plate of ready-made stew.

Esau could have refused Jacob's offer and taken control of the situation as the elder brother, but he was too lazy to prepare his meal. For the temporary convenience of a plate of ready-made stew, Esau gave away his invaluable birthright and everything it came with. He solved a momentary challenge by creating a transgenerational problem for himself and his descendants.

The Striking Resemblance

The story of these two brothers bears a striking resemblance to the story of White and Black people in South Africa and on the African continent at large. As Black people, we are the indigenous inhabitants of this continent. We are the ones with birthright blessings over this continent. Moreover, we have been blessed with the necessary skills to exploit its resources for our benefit and development. With all the minerals buried under our feet, all the fertile land we have, and the many talents of our indigenous people, we were set up for an eternity of blessings – heaven on earth! Literally!

Blacks are the people destined to receive and own the wealth of this land called Africa. We are the possessors of the birthright advantage over this continent. We were never meant to be poor or live in destitution. We were never meant to be used as fund-raising objects by Whites and their western organisations. We were divinely positioned to take hold of the riches of this land and be the envy of the rest of the world. After all, Africa is the richest continent in the world with abundant deposits of gold, diamonds, platinum, copper, lithium, cobalt, bauxite, oil, gas, coal and the many other minerals that all other continents wish they had.

> *For the temporary convenience of a plate of ready-made stew, Esau gave away his invaluable birthright and everything it came with. He solved a momentary challenge by creating a transgenerational problem for himself and his descendants.*

Africa is Our God-given Inheritance

We are the firstborn of Africa and indeed of South Africa. We were in a position like that of Esau. We were destined for greater things for generations to come; only had we been shrewd and discerning in our dealings with White people from the get-go.

When the Europeans came to our shores for the very first time, they found us right here, in this country, and on this continent. But just like Jacob, they were quick to negotiate unscrupulous deals with our ancestors to our detriment. White people even went to the extent of forcibly and violently dispossessing us of our land and livestock. The deals were made with our ancestors, but we still bear the brunt many generations later. We do not have the details of the day-to-day events that took place in those ancient times. History does not account for that. However, based on mere research, observation and the outcomes of those negotiations, we can safely conclude that Black people exchanged their God-given inheritance and birthright blessings for the convenience of plates of ready-made stew offered to them by White people. Thus, Black people can be likened to Esau, humble as doves but stupid as sheep going to the slaughter, and white people to Jacob, shrewd as serpents and ruthless as wolves.

> *Blacks are the people destined to receive and own the wealth of this land called Africa. We are the possessors of the birthright advantage over this continent*

The Undeniable Truth

What we know for sure is that a lot of cheating and stealing took place each time these two groups came face to face. In the end, Black people lost their birthright to the crafty Whites who cleverly deceived and manipulated them. They forcefully took our land and its wealth from us through an evil and diabolical process called colonisation. Furthermore, they forced us to serve them as their slaves and servants for meagre wages. Ultimately, they went on to enjoy all the blessings listed in Isaac's coronation speech to Jacob:

"May God give you heaven's dew and the earth's richness and an abundance of grain and new wine. May nations serve you and people bow down to you. Be lord over your brothers and may the sons of your mother bow down to you. May those who curse you be cursed, and those who bless you be blessed."

As for us Black people, we continually face the fate of Esau – a hopeless, desolate and dependent destiny. I am sure you are noticing this striking similarity.

All the things that were erroneously given to Jacob are the exact things White people in our country enjoy today at the expense of Black people.

White Privilege vs Black Marginalisation

Jacob was told that he will not serve anyone but will be served by Esau.

To this day, White people do not serve Black people; but Black people, who are the vast majority, serve White people, who are the minority. It will remain like this for centuries to come if we do not engage in a people-driven revolution to address this structural injustice. A revolution that begins in the mind of the Black person you see every day in the mirror.

> *We were divinely positioned to take hold of the riches of this land and be the envy of the rest of the world.*

Jacob was also told the riches of the earth would belong to him.

To this day, between 67% and 72% of land in South Africa – which is rich in vast minerals, arable and fertile land for growing quality crops and vegetation, populated by variations of wildlife and all its discovered and undiscovered wealth – is owned and controlled by White people.

Jacob was told he would have an abundance of grain and new wine.

To this day, White people in South Africa own the means of production; their companies are the ones producing the food we eat, the drinks we consume, the clothes we wear, and the wine we export from the Western Cape. Our local industries are under the firm grip of White people, and like Jacob, they are in full control.

Jacob was made lord over his brother.

To this day, White people boss around Black people. Black brothers and sisters may not agree with this, but it is and will be our sad reality until we *"grow restless and throw this yoke from off our necks"*.

> *To this day, White people do not serve Black people; but Black people, who are the vast majority, serve White people, who are the minority. It will remain like this for centuries to come if we do not engage in a people-driven revolution to address this structural injustice.*

Same WhatsApp Group

The deceit of White people to Black people resembles the deceit of Jacob to Esau. White people deceitfully stole resources from our ancestors and own them even to this day. On the other hand, what Esau – the defrauded one – ended up with, is a true reflection of the plight of Black people to this day. As sad and heart-breaking this is, it is the harsh reality we face, and one we must work tirelessly to overturn for the sake of our children, our grandchildren, and our great-grandchildren.

Future generations of Black people should not inherit the mess and the despondency that we find ourselves in. God forbid!

Now, let's investigate what happened to someone who sold his birthright.

Esau was told that his dwelling would be far away from the productive land.

To this day, Black people's homelands and living spaces are great distances away from the rich land on which our cities and mines are built. Everywhere in South Africa, Black people must travel long distances to arrive in the rich areas of this country. We were relegated to occupying the desolate lands in our own country – where in some cases our people have no access to arable land, running water, electricity, proper roads and infrastructure. Decent health care services are also a great distance away from most of our people who need to access the health care system. It appears the so-called benefits of colonisation as expressed by Hellen Zille when she tweeted, *"For those claiming (the) legacy of colonialism was ONLY negative, think of our independent judiciary, transport infrastructure, piped water etc.",* are still a long way away from our people. To this day, Black people in rural and informal settlements of South Africa struggle to access running water, internet connectivity, and proper infrastructure.

> *The deceit of White people to Black people resembles the deceit of Jacob to Esau. White people deceitfully stole resources from our ancestors and own them even to this day*

Turnaround Is Possible

Towards the end of the painful speech by Isaac, Esau was told that only when he grew tired and restless of the heavy yoke the master (his brother) had put around his neck, would he be able to remove it and throw it away. This is an important point to which I will return to later in this book.

My fellow Black people, our situation is like that of Esau, as depicted in Genesis chapter 27 in the Bible. The negotiations between the indigenous Black people of Africa and the colonial Whites from Europe ended with us losing significantly and Whites gaining by defrauding us.

Today, many centuries later, we are still lamenting the considerable losses from our stupidity when dealing with White people. What is even more painful is that this pattern continues unabated to this day. As a people, we are agitated by this unchallenged status quo, but we are still generally clueless about what we need to do to recover what rightfully belongs to us. This struggle requires us to be courageous and decisive. We need to unite and fight with relentless passion until we achieve the goal of breaking the yoke of our erstwhile masters from our necks so that we can be key players in the mainstream economy of our country. We cannot continue being the helpless consumers we have been all along. Something must give! We must fight this battle and break this yoke until the results of this great injustice and trickery against us are reversed.

The Restlessness

The social unrest, bitter political rhetoric, and demands for expropriation of land without compensation, nationalisation of banks and mines stem from the dissatisfaction with the majority of South African wealth being in the hands of the minority. All friction between Blacks and Whites is caused by this emotive issue and White people must be willing to share the wealth they possess with Black people – since it was stolen from under the Black man's feet. The tensions continue to grow even after twenty-seven years of liberation, and I do not see them easing any time soon.

> *We need to unite and fight with relentless passion until we achieve the goal of breaking the yoke of our erstwhile masters from our necks so that we can be key players in the mainstream economy of our country.*

The only way we are going to effectively redress the inequalities caused by apartheid is by rejecting the unacceptable norm and refusing to be classified as a secondary race or as inferior citizens in our own country. We must become restless over the issues that affect us and the future of our posterity as a race. For it is only then, that we will break the White man's yoke and push towards economic and cultural self-determination.

> *We must fight this battle and break this yoke until the results of this great injustice and trickery against us are reversed.*

The Curse of Ready-Made Stew

What is widening the wealth gap between Blacks and Whites, you may wonder?

The truth is, it is our continued reliance and dependence on White people for ready-made stew over the centuries, which has grown even worse since the liberation of Black people in South Africa in 1994. Instead of seeing freedom as an opportunity to restore our dignity and pride and start preparing our own stew, we once again sold our birthright and destiny to the White people for the convenience of another plate of ready-made stew. In so doing, we continue to propel them further ahead of us and have allowed them to increase their grip on the many things that we should have taken control of from the onset. We have become more and more accustomed to the convenience of these plates of ready-made stew that we were getting from them that we never cared about preparing our own. Foolish and unaware of the White man's agenda, we proceeded to mortgage more of our birthright inheritance to them in exchange for more plates of ready-made stew. Today we celebrate their residential developments, schools, malls and franchises in our townships, forgetting that we are killing our local economies and enriching theirs in the process. Little do we realise that we are losing our major competitive advantage over them – our pride, birthright, land, dignity and inheritance, all for a meagre plate of ready-made stew.

I know you are wondering what this ready-made stew might be. Just hang in there, it will unfold as we journey on.

> *The only way we are going to effectively redress the inequalities caused by apartheid is by rejecting the unacceptable norm and refusing to be classified as a secondary race or as inferior citizens in our own country.*

The Root of Our Mess

The problem we are sitting with here is that we have allowed ourselves to become lazy. Instead of using the freedom our ancestors painfully fought for to develop ourselves and our communities, we exchanged it for the conveniences offered by the White man. We traded our ancestors' tears, sweat and blood for a White man's poisonous plate of conveniences.

We misunderstood liberation and saw it as an opportunity to integrate with Whites. We were so eager to partake of the so-called benefits of this integration that we never made plans to cook our own stews by developing our township communities, our schools, our businesses, our franchises, our healthcare facilities and the economies within black townships. This lack of foresight allowed White people to wield greater power and influence over us and continue as our *"lords"*, to quote the old man Isaac.

At the core of our myriad problems is the lack of self-love. We do not love ourselves enough to roll up our sleeves, get down to work, rebuild from the ground up, and in the process, cook our own stews. We fear that it is too much work that may take too long to accomplish. We perceive benefitting from White's people's establishments as advancement and progress; on the contrary, we are regressing and reinforcing the fallacy of white supremacy. We are giving White people our souls in exchange for their plates of ready-made stews. This is exactly what Esau was ignorant of when he gave his birthright away. He reckoned that the work involved was too time consuming and strenuous. Therefore, out of desperation, he chose the convenient path of exchanging eternal value for temporal relief, and he paid dearly for it. How stupid was that?

> *Instead of using the freedom our ancestors painfully fought for to develop ourselves and our communities, we exchanged it for the conveniences offered by the White man. We traded our ancestors' tears, sweat and blood for a White man's poisonous plate of conveniences.*

Unpacking the Plate of Ready-Made Stew

In this context, the plate of ready-made stew refers to the dependence of Black people on White people for our daily sustenance. An obvious example is the staples we consume such as bread and mealie meal. Black people are undoubtedly the biggest consumers of these, yet, after twenty-seven years of freedom, democracy and liberation, we still rely on White people to produce, distribute and bring these basic consumables to our doorsteps – items which we can without doubt produce ourselves. White people did not invent mealie meal, we did. But because of laziness, we stupidly gave this industry away to the White man without even thinking twice – the hopeless Esau spirit!

Are we saying that after more than twenty-seven years of liberation, we still cannot produce the mealie meal and bread that we consume, and the clothes we wear? Do we still need to be clothed by White people even today?

A plate of ready-made stew refers to the general comfort we receive from watching White people lead the economy while we tag along as hopeless consumers, laden with a survival mentality, continually struggling to make ends meet as though we are physically and mentally incapable of cooking our own stews.

> *White people did not invent mealie meal, we did. But because of laziness, we stupidly gave this industry away to the White man without even thinking twice – the hopeless Esau spirit!*

Give Us Each Day Our Daily Stew

Think of the many trucks driving into townships every morning, delivering bread to millions of black households. One would have thought that with Black people comprising the bulk of consumers, especially after twenty-seven years of liberation, we would have identified this opportunity and started our own bakeries. This is not a difficult business to venture into. It is not rocket science to develop a bread recipe, bake, package the bread and distribute it. But because we are too accustomed to ready-made stew or in this case, ready-made bread **(Sphathlo or Kota)**, we are comfortable watching money exit our communities daily to our impoverishment and detriment. How stupid are we that we fail to see such a glaring opportunity staring at us like an owl?

Hai kona man! Refeteletse!

This is too much!

> *We were never meant to be poor, nor were we meant to be living in destitution, or be used as fund-raising objects for whites and their western organizations.*

They Made It by Working What is Ours

When I say White people took what rightfully belonged to Black people, I do not mean that White people did not work for what they have. Of course, they worked hard for it but they did so on stolen land. White people organised themselves and capitalised on the Black man's hard labour to get to where they are today – just as Jacob had to be diligent for the blessings conferred on him by his father to be realised. Jacob benefited where Esau was supposed to have benefited, just as White people continually benefit where Black people should be benefitting. When White people arrived here and in the centuries following their arrival, they did the work that was supposed to have been conceived and pioneered by Black people. The real issue here is not about hard work, but about how like Esau, we have made it ridiculously easy for the White man to get ahead of us because we lack discernment and shrewdness in transacting with them. Therefore, they are the ones extracting the bountiful mineral resources buried under our feet, while the indigenous Black people serve them as cheap labour, and we dare call that progress and development.

Sadly, even though we are the rightful heirs of the land and its wealth, our people did not pioneer the work that took place on our soil. They were only brought in as cheap labourers, while the White minority derived the fruit and benefit of our blood, sweat, tears, indigenous knowledge, livestock and land. Even today, Black people are still struggling to earn a living as they continue working for White people in exchange for peanuts.

What is also saddening is that we seem to function at optimum only when we are brought in to provide labour under the leadership and ownership of White people in their companies. However, when working by ourselves we are slack, lazy and unproductive. This is a sign of our self-hate, self-disapproval and outright stupidity.

Life Before the Raw Deal

Esau lived well before his fateful plate of stew transaction with Jacob. Everything was going well for him. He was his father's favourite son. Treasures and blessings were waiting for him to receive. He was a skilful hunter. He was resourceful, neither destitute nor poor. But see what a measly plate of ready-made stew cost him – his illustrious destiny and that of his generations yet unborn.

Similarly, our people were also dignified and self-reliant before they undiscerningly negotiated with Whites. We have neither heard of nor read reports that they used to die of starvation or hunger back in those centuries. They were talented and skilled in their own way. They had plenty of food, land, and livestock, and from that, they were able to sufficiently sustain themselves. Not only that, but they also ran viable economies which included mining and sophisticated construction. Then, just like Esau, they sheepishly entertained the trickster, and the rest is history.

Lessons From This Story

The story of Jacob and Esau teaches us that seeking temporary relief from desperation can cost your fortune and legacy, while a little endurance and inconvenience can open doors to an even greater fortune for generations to come. To this day, Black people are still desperately seeking momentary relief from White people at the expense of future generations. We still knock on their doors begging for employment so that every month we could survive from a plate of ready-made stew – a dish that we are well capable of cooking for ourselves. Compromised by naivety, we fail to see that our addiction to ease, comfort and convenience keeps us under the White man's yoke of economic slavery and oppression.

We do not want to pioneer our own work. We behave as though without White people we are crippled, dysfunctional and doomed. On the other hand, the White man is aggressively advancing his cause towards further economic dominance and wealth generation. The wrongful recipients of

Africa's blessings are still prospering from Africa's wealth while most of those for whom the inheritance was reserved live in abject poverty, suffering and desolation. How sad and pitiful is this?

Somebody, kindly pass me a handkerchief. I need to wipe the tears from my eyes. This is too painful and heartbreaking! *Mathata*!

> *The story of Jacob and Esau teaches us that seeking temporary relief from desperation can cost your fortune and legacy, while a little endurance and inconvenience can open doors to an even greater fortune for generations to come.*

This Must Stop

Listen to me, Black man, this trajectory needs to be disrupted now! We must challenge and stretch ourselves to be self-sustaining. We must learn to start our work from ground zero, if we must, and endure the ensuing temporary pain and suffering; knowing that we will be rewarded with transgenerational liberty and prosperity. If we still allow Whites to be in control of the mainstream economy, we will owe them our lives. Our children, grandchildren and future generations of Black people will be indebted to them as well. We cannot continue to be comfortable with this status quo. This norm is not acceptable at all. The yoke must be broken as a matter of urgency, and it begins with us becoming agitated and restless against the dominant mindset of convenience and dependency within the Black nation.

> *We do not want to pioneer our own work. We behave as though without White people we are crippled, dysfunctional and doomed.*

In subsequent chapters, we will expand the practical examples of ready-made stew, but for now you have enough to get you thinking long, deep and hard.

"Don't care where you come from, as long as you are a black man, you are an African."

Peter Tosh

The yoke must be broken as a matter of urgency, and it begins with us becoming agitated and restless against the dominant mindset of convenience and dependency within the Black nation.

2

CULTURAL STUPIDITY

"Is it right that a man should abandon his mother tongue for someone else's? It looks like a dreadful betrayal and produces a guilty feeling. But for me, there is no other choice. I have been given a language and I intend to use it."

Chinua Achebe

Relinquishing our economic birthright and inheritance was not difficult for us because we had already betrayed our own identity and heritage as a people in our misguided pursuit of whiteness. For us, it never rains, it pours!

Language

Have you ever observed that across Europe, White people have always jealously protected their languages, heritage and culture? They have established systems and institutions that ensure the preservation and perpetuation of their languages, cultures, heritage and history. They always speak German in Germany as much as they always speak Spanish in Spain. The Greeks will never stop speaking their language in Greece and Portuguese will forever be the official language of business and instruction in Portugal. All government business and learning in England is conducted in English. Italian families in Italy speak Italian at home as much as the French do French. This is common practice in all self-respecting and self-asserting nations and cultures.

The same self-respecting nations and cultures have even gone as far as preserving their way of preparing food, their general lifestyles and traditions, which they proudly pass on to future generations. In the East, the same trend is observable. If you observe countries like Japan, South Korea and China, you will notice how their presidents do not even bother speaking English when they host English-speaking presidents. They use the services of interpreters while they stick to their languages. Such is the respect, honour and pride they attach to their languages. Why then do Black South Africans humiliate government officials when they fail to speak English "properly" and "eloquently" or should I say when they do not speak in a British and/or an American accent? Have we forgotten that our legendary icon, the late Rolihlahla Nelson Madiba Mandela, was highly respected globally, even though he spoke English with a heavy and thick Xhosa accent?

The Truth Hurts

I am certain that at this point, I have already provoked many who might say, "Africa was colonised and enslaved, these Eastern countries were not." Others might even argue that foreign languages were imposed on us as Africans and that we did not voluntarily abandon our languages in pursuit of English, Portuguese or French. True, Africa was colonised, and we had other languages forcefully thrust upon us – that is an undeniable fact. However, is that not reason enough for us to be determined to change those things that affect our pride and dignity as a people? Shouldn't we as Africans stand up and decide to restore and reinforce our damaged languages and integrate them into our daily lives, education and economy? Whose responsibility should it be to promote and preserve *Setswana, IsiZulu, IsiXhosa, XiTsonga, SeSotho, IsiNdebele, Sepedi, Swati,* and *TshiVenda*?

The only way a nation can affirm itself and attain collective power is by loving and protecting its identity, languages and cultures; as well as by using them to build national pride and carve a distinct brand for themselves within the community of nations.

Stupidity Must Fall

Black South Africans want to be respected as a race but are trying to achieve this by doing all the wrong things and ignoring all the things they should be doing to be taken seriously. We despise and neglect our languages and then we slam white Afrikaners when they stand up to fight for theirs. We perceive Afrikaners defending their language as an affront to us and a gesture of outright rejection of us. We react with fury when other races fight for a cause they believe in. I am of the view that in all fairness, Afrikaners are right to protect their Afrikaans language; after all, it is theirs to protect and promote. We as Africans should be doing the same regarding our respective languages. It is the honourable thing for any race to do. Keep going Afrikaners, keep going, *gaan maar aan*! I agree with you on this one!

Please do not get me wrong, I understand the discomfort Black people feel when Afrikaners impose their language. White people oppressed and violated us using their language and maybe their language has become a symbol of oppression. But it is their language after all; the one they should be allowed to speak freely, with pride and dignity. Let us, therefore, allow them the freedom to defend and protect it.

What we should be agitated over is the marginalisation and relegation of our languages to the periphery by ourselves. We should be aggrieved by our willingness to actively participate in the genocide of our languages. We should be challenged to restore them into the mainstream of our lives. We must rise and passionately promote our languages more aggressively than the Afrikaners are defending theirs. We should be focused on what matters to us, lest our languages become endangered species to be read about in cultural museums a few generations from now.

Languages were created by God and given to us all as unique ways to express our humanity and diversity. We should be jealously guarding and protecting the gifts that God gave to us with our lives if need be. Languages are tools that we have been given for communication, but they also serve as carriers of history and culture.

As I already mentioned, there is only one way a nation can affirm itself, and that is by using its native languages in day-to-day interactions and business affairs. When you use your language you affirm your originality and you carve out your own unique identity in the global community. We need to start doing that as African people.

As Black people in South Africa, we have lost our mark everywhere. We are happy to have our identities scorned and our cultures relegated to the periphery. We have not even attempted to have our languages instituted as primary media of instruction in our education system as the Afrikaners have done. While this is partly because of the oppression and marginalisation that we were subjected to for many years during the evil apartheid regime, we have still failed to start a long-overdue revolutionary recovery process despite having the power to do so. We have failed to initiate such a process because we are a divided people whose opinions are scattered. We lack common agreement around issues that concern our development, advancement and destiny as a people. Our lack of collaborative skills is our main weakness.

> *What we should be agitated over is the marginalisation and relegation of our languages to the periphery by ourselves.*

Black Man, Why?

Why are we the only group of people who work hard to ensure that our children have no mastery of their mother tongues? Why do we feel such a great sense of pride when our children cannot even speak their indigenous languages in their daily interactions? Why are we the only race that finds happiness in pushing our children towards whiteness and numbing their blackness? As if that was not bad enough, we even have the audacity and madness to brag about it. What a shame! *"Ngwanake o tsena sekolo sa makgowa, o bolela English le Afrikaans fela."* What a shame!

Lest We Forget

During the June 1976 Soweto uprising, our bold and courageous young people were killed for protesting the use of Afrikaans as the medium of instruction in black schools. The youth of 1976 had an appreciation of the power of language. Fast-forward to 2021, Black parents are voluntarily and proudly taking their children to formerly whites-only schools where they learn Afrikaans – schools where our languages are neither taught nor spoken; instead, they are trodden underfoot.

This is a direct insult to the youth who sacrificed their lives on that crucial day in June 1976! How can Black children who are living in a time of freedom still be studying Afrikaans at the expense of their own indigenous languages and be proud thereof?

Whichever way you look at it, there is no way you can dignify this shameful reality. Our languages have neither protectors nor advocates because we have lost our pride and dignity as a people. They have become utterly defenceless.

Hector Pieterson is, without a doubt, turning in his grave!

> *Languages were created by God and given to us all as unique ways of expressing our humanity and diversity.*

Where is Our Pride?

There is a prevalent phenomenon in our nation today that I would like to caution you of. Whenever a black family earns a decent level of income, they are quick to scramble for every possible opportunity to integrate with White people. Slowly but surely, they abandon their languages as they aspire to appear and sound white and thoughtlessly stray away from who they truly are.

Integration and association with White people and their cultures seem to thrill us. We perceive these as upgrades or promotions from being an inferior Black person to the level of being a pseudo-superior White. From being Black to being *amper baas* and *amper miesies. Ja! Amper maar nie stamper nie.* We have set whiteness and proximity to it as a standard that we aspire towards because we believe this improves our sense of self-worth and causes us to feel better about ourselves. In so doing, we have afflicted ourselves and have ingrained within our subconscious minds this false and misguided notion of black inferiority and white supremacy.

Let us Consider Our Ways and Be Wise

When we move our children to white schools and start communicating with them in English within our own homes, *yebo, emakhaya wethu,* we dissociate ourselves from the very things that define us and connect us to our roots. Look at how shameful we are; we neither read nor write books in our languages. By so doing, we are depriving our children of their unique identity and languages. Instead, we are solidifying the madness and pathetic notion that African languages are backward and inferior. By not using our African languages, we give English a superior status – *to counter this, I will make sure that this book is translated into as many African languages as possible.*

My beloved Black people, let me break the truth down to you. English is a language, just like any other language. There is absolutely nothing superior about the English language, **asseblief tog, bathong, sho**! To think that a white language is better than any black language is madness! For goodness' sake, a white language is just another language! There is nothing special about English. Such folly of thought that elevates white languages above black languages only exists because we have allowed it for far too long. We must address this stupidity head-on before we lose our heritage as quickly as we did our birthright. It is time we learned from the foolishness of our past and change our ways, Black man! Either that or we lose whatever remnants of our blackness we have left. As the saying goes, *"If you do not learn from your history, you are doomed."*

> ***There is absolutely nothing superior about the English language.***

No Moral High Ground

I have realised that a language can only gain prominence and respect when its speakers come forward to promote it and entrench it within their communities as a way of life. Now tell me, why have we not come full circle to promote our languages by using them in meetings where there are no English speakers? Why are we not entrenching our languages in our daily economic activities? The simple answer is this, we are shameless hypocrites who apply double standards whenever it suits us. We scream about White people undermining us and our cultures, yet we are the ones at the forefront of undermining our own cultures and languages by always defaulting to

English, even when there is no need for us to do so. We can never justifiably take the moral high ground on this issue and protest the marginalisation of our languages because we are the guilty ones on this matter. We are the ones who single-handedly decimate our languages. The Afrikaners, on the other hand, can take the moral high ground on the issue of language because they will never speak to another Afrikaner in English. *Nooit nie! Lingawa licoshwe yizinkukhu!*

Black Power is Real

Black people are the powerhouse of this nation and its economy. Remember how we pushed for the collapse of the apartheid regime? That is a simple reflection of the power we have. We however rarely ignite and apply it. The day we decide to, we will successfully lobby for whatever we want and succeed. History has proven so. Our numbers and economic muscle as a race empower us to achieve anything that we demand whenever we put our collective effort behind our resolution.

We can demand that newspapers and magazines be printed in our languages and surely that demand will be met. We can demand that consumer products be labelled in our languages and achieve that too. We can even lobby for the use of our languages in the banking and commercial sectors, and it will be granted. Our numbers, and consequently, our collective capacity is the power we can use to achieve anything we want without *toyi-toying*. There is no need to resort to destructive and regressive mass actions as evidenced in the recent looting of our business hubs in KwaZulu-Natal and Gauteng. Bloody madness!

We are the only race that has the critical mass to lobby against whatever we do not want, press for whatever we desire and get it. This is a weapon we have neither fully explored nor exploited to our detriment and demise.

Of the nine provinces in South Africa, KZN is the only province that circulates prominent newspapers written in an African language, *IsiZulu*. These newspapers are *iLanga* and *iSolezwe*.

In the rest of the provinces, people are deprived of the opportunity to read newspapers in their African languages. I do not know whether we are forced to accept this status quo, or we just prefer the languages of our erstwhile masters above our own. Whichever way you prefer to look at it, we are not promoting our languages and that is despicable. *Sies*! It sucks!

A Small Detour

Imagine if we were to come together as Black people in our massive numbers, galvanised by a renewed sense of self-love and lobby against the allocation of small yards by property developers (endorsed by our local municipalities) to our people in townships. The yards on which these houses are built are so small, that once the house is built, there is no space left to build a car garage. These small yards will never be allocated in a predominantly white residential area. Excuse my silly thinking if you will, but every time I pass through areas where our people are allocated small yards, I cannot help but wonder how our people can enjoy their right to privacy when their yards are so small and close to one another that one can hear the conversations and adult activities taking place next door without straining their ears. Why we stand idly by and watch as this continues unabated? I will never understand!

The white minority developers continue to make a killing by buying land in the townships and ridiculing Black people by selling them small houses on these tiny yards at a premium. From a distance these areas look like concentration camps from the Hitler era.

Come to think of it, as you drive through areas commonly known as poor white residential communities in South Africa, you will notice that as poor as those Whites are and look, the size of the yards allocated to them is more than double the size of the yards in some newly developed black residential areas. I cannot help but think that the apartheid regime did a far better job taking care of its poor Whites than our black government is doing for its marginalised Black communities. This is true with houses that our people must purchase, and even worse with some of the houses under the Reconstruction and Development Programme (RDP). Do you remember the time when Black people were forcefully removed by the apartheid regime from the likes of Sophiatown and Lady Selbourne, and relocated to the present-day black townships like Soweto and Soshanguve? Certainly, you have noticed how the four-roomed houses given by the evil regime are better than the RDP houses built by the black government. What a contrast! What a disappointment!

> *As black people, we are the powerhouse of this nation and its economy.*

Sad and painful as this is, we can change this quickly if we come together in our numbers to lobby against such unfair treatment of our people. The same with languages, if we choose to demand information in our native tongues from the corporate world, we will get it. We can call for prominent consideration and respect for our languages in the education sector, and we will get it. As the majority, we will get whatever we consistently and incessantly demand. However, this can only happen when we realise and focus the power that lies in our significant numbers and begin to exercise it.

We Are Out of Order

It is shocking that we are not calling for the prominent recognition of the unique identities and cultures of Black people. Instead, we are the ones destroying any connection we have to our roots or whatever is left of them. Have we become so "civilised" and "progressive" that we consider reading current affairs in our African languages backward? If so, then the white Afrikaners are very primitive and backward for protesting whenever they feel their language is being undermined. Or have our minds been so effectively colonised that we have forgotten who we are in pursuit of who we are not and will never be? We cannot continue to voraciously consume literature written in a foreign language and work tirelessly towards attaining fluency in this foreign language we call English, while our languages are dying a silent and unnoticed death. We need to restore the lost pride and dignity of our languages. We can start by reading more literature in our African languages; for instance, a novel, the Bible, or something of that sort.

> *We cannot continue to voraciously consume literature written in a foreign language and work tirelessly towards attaining fluency in this foreign language we call English, while our languages are dying a silent and unnoticed death.*

As a black South African, I know all too well about the injustices we suffered during apartheid. I experienced the oppression of Blacks by Whites and I continue to witness the extensive damage this oppression caused on our collective and individual psyches. However, I do not believe it is because of apartheid that we have abandoned our languages, cultures and identity. Our thoughtlessness, self-hate and cultural stupidity are to blame for that, not apartheid.

While we are in this ballpark, I might as well confess. The last time I read any literature in my language, *IsiZulu,* other than the Bible was in 1982 when I completed my matric. Since then, I have never touched a single book in *IsiZulu*. I am ashamed of this and vow to make it right. I mention this deliberately because I know that many can identify with this horrible picture that I have just painted. ***Noma kungathiwani,*** this is shameful – ***uhlazo lodwa lolu. Ke mawaza fela.***

Do you think the same applies to an Afrikaner? I seriously doubt a typical Afrikaner has never read any Afrikaans literature since completing matric. I bet most of us, Blacks, have not read anything in our languages post-matric.

Repeat after me please: *I must be careful lest I become a sick Black man who is equally stupid and continues to fall prey to the false narrative of black inferiority and white superiority!*

Please take the next few moments to digest what you have just read.

We Are Losing Ourselves

Our problems are self-inflicted because we do not take ourselves seriously. We have no respect for our identity and our fellow Black people. We respect everything and everyone that is not black. We have such pathetic self-hate and disgusting sense of apathy towards ourselves. We have developed a deplorable and deep-seated self-hatred; a self-rejection and self-disapproval because we believe the baseless lies that have been told to us by the evil White man in his effort to keep us under his yoke. We have not only bought into the doctrine of black inferiority, but we have also grown to loathe ourselves so much that we are unashamedly willing to sacrifice our dignity on the altar of convenience, even if it means we continue to slide into oblivion and insignificance.

In the coming chapters, we will talk about how we have gone to the extent of putting the interests of other races above our very own because we are the only race that suffers from a chronic form of cultural stupidity, cultural suicide and cultural neglect.

It pains my heart when I observe how thousands of Black parents would rather take their children to schools that are managed by White people than a school managed by Black people. What many of these black parents conveniently ignore is that in these white schools, white culture is instilled in their children, and African languages and cultures have no recognition whatsoever. They do this in the name of exposing their children to quality education. I do not agree with this idea of sacrificing our heritage and pride to expose our children to whiteness. Instead, I believe that we should come together, speak with one voice, raise the standard of excellence in our township schools and make them attractive to other Black parents and the rest of the world. We should be having conversations around how we can educate our children on our terms, so our languages and cultures are given the prominence they deserve. We should be about building schools that promote the dignity of our race, languages and cultures, and not selling the souls of our children in exchange for a "quality" education that betrays our roots and identity.

We cannot continue to trade our destiny because we are too lazy to cook our stews, though we have all the ingredients we need to cook up a storm. We can do it, **bafowethu**! Let us get together and do this for our race, our heritage and our rich languages. In the process, we will earn the respect of our children and grandchildren. We should not produce children who are like mules, neither horses nor donkeys, but *'coconuts'* whose only connection to their identity is their brown skin, which some have come to despise, hence the bleaching culture that we see today. I promise you our ancestors will be proud of us for doing this. They will toast to some African beer (***mbamba or*** *mqombothi*) in celebration of us finally waking up. This double consciousness must end here and now!

Please take a deep breath, put the book down for a few minutes and take time to reflect or take a walk before you proceed because this is going to be deep.

Here we go again.

> *We are the only race that suffers from a chronic form of cultural stupidity, cultural suicide and cultural neglect.*

If They Were Us

If white Afrikaners were in the same predicament that we find ourselves in, and if we were to be in their privileged situation, do you think that they would take their children to our "top-tier" black schools and institutions? Do you think they would allow themselves to bow to our cultures and languages? Of course not, they would never sink to such a low level and take their children to black schools, never! Not in a million centuries! White people are too proud of who they are and too deeply entrenched in their roots to do so. They would never betray their heritage and culture as we do.

Can you imagine Afrikaner families encouraging their children to learn *IsiZulu* and English at an elite black school that does not give their language prominent recognition? Can you imagine a very educated and rich Afrikaner family residing in Houghton or Waterkloof, conversing with their children in *IsiZulu* or English for that matter? It has never happened! It is not happening! And it will never happen! **Dit gaan nooit gebeur nie! Dit sal die dag wees!** Yet you will find our black middle-class parents forcing the English language down their children's throats and brainwashing them with this foolish aspiration of tirelessly trying to get closer and closer to being white while drifting further and further away from being black and beautiful. This is sickening! There is nothing as pathetic as seeing a Black child who cannot relate to their blackness because they have been brainwashed by their Black parents and white schools to elevate whiteness and to despise blackness to the point where the child cannot even pronounce their African names properly. *Lafa elihle kakhulu!*

We are raising a generation of culturally stupid Black children who cannot converse with their grandparents because they can only speak English and Afrikaans while their grandparents only speak an African language. Shame on us! Shame on you, Black man! Have we degenerated to such low levels of cultural stupidity? This is sad, Black man. It is shameful and sad indeed. What a loathsome development to watch, enough to cause one to puke. I feel nauseous as I write these words.

Black parents are producing black "coconuts" who think they will evolve into becoming white. What they do not realise is that *"once a Pirate, always a Pirate"*; once a Black man, always a Black man. Your white accent, blonde hair and your white "Oh

My God" (*OMG*) gestures can never erase your blackness. Black man, it is time you accepted that you were born black, and you will die black. There is no escape from that. Therefore, I call you to love being black, love blackness and everything that is connected to it, and pass that black pride and self-love on to your children.

A Quick Indaba

Let us be brutally honest with each other for a moment. Wouldn't it be an unpardonable disgrace within the Afrikaner bloodline if an Afrikaner child was unable to read, write or communicate proficiently in his language? You have a better chance of finding snow in hell than finding an Afrikaner child who cannot converse in Afrikaans. This is the kind of pride we need to restore to ourselves and to instil in our children. We must rise and reclaim our position. It begins with reviving our pride and celebrating the majestic beauty of our African languages, cultures and heritage - ***ubuntu.***

> *We should be about building schools that promote the dignity of our race, languages, and cultures, and not selling the souls of our children in exchange for a 'quality' education that betrays our roots and identity.*

A Look at the Other Side

Afrikaners have movements such as *Afriforum, Solidariteid,* and *Afrikaner Broederbond,* which uncompromisingly and unashamedly protect and promote the interests of the Afrikaner culture, language and heritage. Therefore, if Afrikaners were in our disgraceful situation of dependence, they would be quick to mobilise and galvanise to build their institutions, even without the help of the government. They would do whatever it takes to ensure their pride remains intact. They would never settle for a plate of ready-made stew from Black people. The only ready-made stew they would ever accept from Black people is our service to them as cheap labourers. In their eyes, menial work is fit for the inferior Blacks, not for them. They would cook their own stew regardless of the challenges that they would face in doing so. They would never be apologetic about putting their race first in all that they do. Truth be told, I crave their sense of pride for our Black South Africans and Africans on the entire continent. How I wish we had this attitude towards our cultures, heritage and languages.

"Heaven help the black man", as Brooke Benton would sing.

How They Did It

After taking over from British rule, the Afrikaners formed what was known as the *Afrikaner Broederbond*. The primary purpose of the *Afrikaner Broederbond* was to capacitate the Afrikaner community with enough skills to run the country without the need for external assistance. They were intentional and purposeful about having an adequate supply of medical doctors, engineers, accountants, plumbers, teachers, nurses and every other skill necessary for their advancement and dominance. They were determined to build an economy with an infrastructure that would empower them for supremacy and affirm their own culture and identity as sovereign. This they achieved without sacrificing their language on the altar of convenience. All these professionals were taught in their indigenous language, Afrikaans. I wonder why we allow ourselves to be so sloppy and carefree on such a destiny defining matter that epitomizes the essence of who we are, as created by the Almighty God. Why do we settle for being cheap copies instead of being proud to be the genuine originals we were fearfully and wonderfully made to be?

Fast forward to 2021, the system of apartheid has collapsed and democracy is now a reality in South Africa, yet the Afrikaners will not back down from their agenda of maintaining their sense of originality as a race and protecting their language and culture. Organisations like *Afriforum* will remain relevant as they continue to fight for the protection and preservation of white privilege at all costs.

What About Us?

Who is promoting black interests? Do we even see ourselves as worthy of our birthright identity? Or have we become so content with the stew we are being served by the white minority that we have ceased to care about our pride and dignity? Black man here is an urgent matter that we must attend to. We can no longer sit by and watch our cultures, languages and heritage dissipate because we choose to relegate ourselves to a state of insignificance and irrelevance. Our attempts at integrating into a foreign culture that does not even tolerate us only expose our folly. Our obsession with whiteness and proximity to whatever it represents cannot go unchallenged and unchanged. It is about time we started embracing the reflection that we see in the mirror, rather than trying to manipulate it in favour of whiteness.

God loves you as you are, my Black brother, especially you my Black sister, stop rejecting who you are in favour of who you will never be. Just as the Apostle Paul says, *"The whole world awaits the manifestation of the sons of God"* (Romans 8:19). God and the whole world await the manifestation of your black beauty and the manifold expression of your enhanced black elegance.

We now need to be more innovative about how we can present our beauty without accessorising ourselves with fake hair from Brazil, Malaysia, Peru and China as if there is something inferior about our kinky hair. There are boundless styles that we are yet to explore and innovate with our natural hair. May I challenge us to dare to do so. While we are there, let us remember and celebrate our former Miss South Africa and Miss Universe Zozibini Tunzi, who dazzled the world with her natural kinky hair.

This matter of hating black and choosing white is a matter we need to urgently attend to. We need to come together and have some strategic conversations or our race will become culturally extinct on our continent. What an abomination that would be!

It is my heartfelt desire that we, as Black people, would cultivate a mindset like that of the Afrikaners'. With enough people who are willing to fight for, protect and promote our languages, heritage, culture and interests, I am confident we will get there sooner than later!

I believe that as we rekindle the flames of our black pride and remind each other that we are a beautiful people – who are significant and should be in charge of their destiny and self-determination – we will, in tandem, cultivate a mindset stronger than that of the Afrikaners with ease. This will propel us into our rightful place as the powerhouse of this nation and its economy. *Amandla!*

Yes, to Blackness!

Whenever Afrikaner professors converge, they converse in Afrikaans. *Hulle praat met mekaar.*

When black professors who speak the same language meet, they converse in English. They speak, *abakhulumi,* they speak! *Ga ba bolele,* they speak!

The reason they choose English over a common African language is this: they erroneously view English as a measure of intelligence, social status and sophistication. Mastery and artistry of their beautiful African languages are associated with ignorance and backwardness. Imagine, rich languages like *isiZulu, TshiVenda, Sepedi, XiTsonga, SeSotho, Setswana, isiXhosa, SiSwati* and *IsiNdebele* being viewed as symbols of backwardness.

English: A Business Tool

On the other hand, Afrikaners will only use English as a business tool for communicating with people who do not speak their language. After that, they revert to Afrikaans as their default language.

That is all that English must be used for: a tool for doing business globally – not for demonstrating sophistication, intelligence or social status. Stick to your languages, Black man, and only choose to speak the White man's languages when it makes business sense.

One thing you cannot take away from the Afrikaner community is their sense of pride, respect and passion for who they are. They are determined to cement their language in the greater scheme of things in this country, whether we like it or not. They do not give a rip about what we think or do! Our opinions and feelings towards them and their language matter nothing to them.

Their attitude should force us to think twice. How is it that a minority group of White people can be intentional in asserting their language and culture better than the indigenous majority? Shouldn't we be pioneers and champions of the same for our languages and cultures, seeing that we are the vast majority? Are we going to continue to take it lying down and doing nothing about promoting our cultures and languages? If yes, then shame on us! May history judge us ruthlessly for such stupidity and passivity.

Morena boloka setjaba sa heso.

> *...lest we produce children who are like mules; neither horses nor donkeys but 'coconuts' whose only connection to their identity is their brown skin, but their inside is very white...*

Afrikaner Pride *vs* Black Inferiority

The Afrikaner race appreciates that through the promotion of their language they assert themselves as an authentic people. They will never allow their language to be diluted or marginalised. They are very passionate about preserving their place in the community of nations and are known for going to great lengths to protect their interests, language and identity. And yet, when a group of educated and accomplished Black people come together in a meeting, all able to speak one or two African languages in common, they choose to conduct the entire meeting in English because they find the language to be more prestigious than their indigenous dialects. What does this say about us, black man?

Reiteration For Emphasis' Sake

If the tables were turned and the Afrikaners found themselves in our position (that is poor and coming from oppression), they would have reacted differently from how we have chosen to react. They would not cower to black supremacy and send their children to a black school to learn *TshiVenda* or *IsiZulu*. Nor would they suck up to black leadership and join black churches *en masse*, hoping to fit in amongst the black elite. Inflated by their deep-seated sense of pride and urgency to restore their position, they would start from the ground and rebuild from the rubble. Battered and bruised by black oppression, they would continue to speak their language amongst themselves, and slowly establish schools that push their Afrikaner agenda, and begin their resurrection one step at a time until they rise to significance. Our argument for doing the opposite because of colonisation and apartheid does not hold water. It is a pathetic excuse rooted in laziness and love for plates of ready-made stew!

We, as Black people, must break away from that mindset and rise to determine our destiny and the kind of legacy we want to leave for our children. We cannot afford to pass on such stupidity to the next generation. God forbid! *Hayi khona!*

Black Man! Wake Up!

It is time to channel our energies towards rebuilding our communities and addressing the ills our people face daily. We know what it will take to rebuild our communities, but once again, we are found turning a blind eye to the issues that affect our posterity and race. Instead of choosing to build, we are quick to settle for the convenience of a plate of ready-made stew presented to us by White people because we do not value ourselves enough to hold on to our birthright. We are ever ready to be neutralised integration with Whites.

We should be building our schools that model the epitome of black excellence; conversely, we are opting for the ready-made schools that have been built to promote and sustain the interests of the Afrikaner agenda. The white schools we prefer are not designed to elevate our children. The problem is we have not woken up to that truth.

Instead of us building strong enviable black churches, here we are, falling over each other as we run *en masse* to join White people in their ready-made, air-conditioned, wall-to-wall carpeted churches. Churches in which we are not considered important at all, but just because it is white-led, Black people want to be a part of it. This is appalling! It is disappointing that after over twenty-seven years of freedom, the Black man still sees himself as inferior to the White man. How I pray for the eyes of the Black man to be opened. After twenty-seven years of freedom, the Black man still finds a sense of significance by being in the shadow of the White man. We shall speak more about this in the coming chapters.

> *That is all that English must be used for: a tool for doing business globally – not for demonstrating sophistication, intelligence, or social status.*

Tracing the Root

Let us try to get to the root cause of all this. Have we sold our souls to the point where we are not willing to pay the price for establishing ourselves as a respected people? Have we become so slothful that we will not bother to learn how to cook our own stew? Is it because we would rather avoid the hard work required to develop our languages and identity? What is wrong with us? Are we free or *dom*? From the looks of things, we appear to be more on the *dom* side!

This obsession we have for ready-made stews is so strong in our genes and chromosomes that we find it difficult to put on our overalls, roll up our sleeves, sing *Shosholoza*, and get fully involved in addressing the dysfunctions within our community structures. We need to come together, mobilise each other, bring our minds, skills and resources together, and develop strategies that will get us out of this rut that we find ourselves in.

Please sing along with me as we shake off this yoke of apathy from our necks:

> ***Hey wena MoAfrika,***
> ***kgale o dutse gae,***
> ***tsoga o iketsetse.***
>
> **Sankomota**

Now, please go to your favourite music app and play this song before you proceed.

A Case in Point

Every morning across the length and breadth of South Africa buses, taxis and *bakkies* transport Black children from their homes in black townships to white suburban schools. Black children now constitute the majority in these schools and white children are now the minority. This is because we do not want to do the hard work of building our own reputable institutions like schools, hospitals, universities, and banks within our communities. Instead, we are comfortable looking to White people for their ready-made stews in the form of schools, churches, chain stores, franchises and so forth. White people built these institutions and entities from scratch, with their blood, sweat and tears and have made them attractive and excellent for their people. Sure, it was our hard labour that they exploited but these institutions were not built for the Black man.

It must not surprise us when White people continue to reign supreme in all aspects of our nation. They have put in the hard work to get there. They chose to uphold their pride and dignity as a people and made their own plates of stew. Why can't we learn from them and work hard to build excellent and enviable private schools, as Black people? Our children are now the majority in these white-owned private schools. This means the Black population and its economy are responsible for supporting and sustaining South Africa's private schooling system. The Black man's hard-earned money is driving the expansion and growth of the largely white-owned private school sector. White educators have realised this; hence they are now opening their private schools in our townships. So, why not build our own private schools, where we can teach and promote our languages, culture and identity? *Hayi man,* come on Black man! We cannot continue to argue that we do not have the economic power to build private schools because of apartheid when it is evident that we are the ones propping up all these white-owned private schools.

> *Our obsession with whiteness and proximity to whatever it represents cannot go unchallenged and unchanged.*

If Not Here, Then Where?

Ponder this: If a black man cannot be number one in his own country, South Africa in this case, where will he ever occupy a place of significance and leadership? If we cannot lead and set the agenda in South Africa, where we should be enjoying the birthright privilege and the advantage of being the indigenous majority, where else do we hope to be in the driving seat of our destiny? In Europe? Asia? No ways! Forget it! **Uyahlanya! Jy is mal!** You are crazy!

It is not the lack of money that keeps us under the White man's cultural yoke. It is our lack of pride, vision, passion, cooperation, agreement, commitment and desire to build through sweat and tears. We have a bankruptcy of willpower not money. A wise man once said, *"A vision will never follow money, but money will always follow the vision."* Once our vision for the future is clear, the rands we need to transform our communities will follow us to our black-owned banks.

> *If a black man cannot be number one in his own country, South Africa in this case, where will he ever occupy a place of significance and leadership?*

Black Madness

In 2015, there was a national outcry against racism, after it had emerged that, allegedly, Curro Foundation School, a private school in Roodeplaat, Pretoria, was separating learners based on their race. While this is sickening, the blatant truth is this: White people will always feel that they can do whatsoever they want in their institutions. After all, they have built them with their *"own cash"* for their own use and not for Blacks. We are simply being tolerated because the constitution pressed them into a corner. The reason their actions are rife with overt racist behaviours is that they feel entitled to have things their way. When they built these institutions, it was never to stroke the egos of insecure Black people who are trying so hard to fit in with them. No! These schools are part of a broader agenda to preserve and promote their interests and privilege. White people run these spaces and they have every right to decide what they believe is in the best interests of their children. The opinions of the disgruntled black majority are not their concern. We must learn from that and very fast; or we will forever be the laughingstock of all races, especially the Afrikaners.

When the Curro story broke, the entire Black nation took to social media, and as usual, screamed the despise of Blacks by Whites. We went to town about how they are unrepentant racists bent on protecting white supremacy.

I beg to differ with popular sentiments on this one. It is we, Black people, who do not take ourselves seriously. We forget that White people have no obligation whatsoever to embrace or love us. They are under no compulsion to accept us. Let us break this down a little further so we can expose and confront our insecurities.

- *Why is it so important for us to feel loved by White people?*
- *Why should White people inconvenience themselves so that we can feel welcome in their space?*
- *Why do Black people crave the embrace of White people to disgusting levels of indignity?*
- *Why are Black people so obsessed with white acceptance? Is acceptance by Whites oxygen for Black people? Do you breathe white acceptance?*
- *Why should White people always be under pressure to prove that they have no problem with Black people? Is our collective sense of esteem that low? Even if it were, why should it be the White man's problem?*
- *Why do we desperately yearn for white affirmation?*
- *Why is there always a national outcry when a story about White people's racist tendencies breaks? Shouldn't we already be used to white racist tendencies because it is all we have ever known and experienced?*

Instead of being enraged by the White man's racist attitude towards us, we should be infuriated by the self-hate we have towards our race. We should not care who loves us or who does not. We simply need to love, embrace and honour ourselves. Let us give self-love and self-acceptance a chance and see if we would still be at the forefront of crying out for white acceptance and embrace.

Reality Check

As I mentioned earlier, Black people need to build their institutions of excellence. We need to get into the driving seat of our agenda and start putting our interests first. If we fail to do so, we are going to find ourselves fighting against racism and its shadows until the end of time. Only when we step up to reclaim our lost identity and position can we change narrative of black inferiority and white supremacy. Either that or we shall remain crying victims forever – victims who blame the government for this, that and the other. It is time we took an introspective look at ourselves and correct the foolish ignorance that we habitually display.

> **When they built these institutions, it was never to stroke the egos of insecure Black people who are trying so hard to fit in with them.**

Spoilt Brats

We are a spoilt people. We are clueless about where we should be going and how we are going to get there. We are going about life aimlessly. In case you missed the memo and update, the world does not owe us anything! Granted, we have been victims of ancient slavery, bondage, colonisation, apartheid, economic exclusion and white supremacist ideologies, but aren't we the ultimate masters of our destiny? Don't we have the skills, brains and capacity to pick ourselves up from the ashes and restore our dignity? We owe it to ourselves to rise from the rubble and ashes of our painful past and build enviable hospitals, schools and businesses that will inspire us to reclaim our birthright and position future generations of Black people for significance and leadership. This is how we will liberate ourselves from our agonising history and rise as the great Black people of South Africa and the entire African continent. We owe this to Kwame Nkrumah, Samora Machel, Nelson Mandela, Robert Mugabe, Patrice Lumumba, and Kenneth Kaunda; not to mention *thee* Martin Luther King, *thee* Uhuru Kenyatta, and *thee* Julius Nyerere.

We must move on from the victim mindset that shackles us to our past and take upon ourselves the responsibility of leaving this world in a far better state than the one we found it in. Likewise, we must stop behaving like little spoilt brats and take charge of our destiny so we can change the narrative on the Black nation for the sake of our children, grandchildren, and ten thousand generations to come.

Our Sickening Hypocrisy

As a race whose destiny and legacy are under threat, we should be casting aside our petty differences and coming together behind this common and noble cause. We should be uniting as one race and fighting for our future as a people, but instead, we keep fighting amongst ourselves over trivial matters like tribalism, politics and Afrophobia. How do we become better? Is it by hating a fellow Black brother from a different tribe, political persuasion or country? Have we betrayed ourselves to such a pitiful extent? Look at us, we show no love and affection for each other and yet we demand it from White people. We hold divisive cultural and intelligence stereotypes against each other. We call each other derogatory names based on our tribes and languages. We are forever divided instead of finding common ground, uniting, and fighting for the restoration of the Black man's legacy and dignity.

We have become so deficient in our love and acceptance of one another that it has somewhat become a norm. We see nothing wrong with such nonsense. No one will ever make an outcry about it; it is now acceptable for Black people to hate each other. But strangely, Whites must never dare try hating or disliking a Black man. They must just love us or else we will ship them back to Holland. The *Dromedaris, Reijer* and *Goede Hoop* which brought Jan Van Riebeck to Africa are waiting for them at the Cape shores.

Whether White people love us or not should be of no substantial consequence to us. We should not even care! The uncomfortable question we must ask ourselves is, do we love ourselves enough to honour and respect each other as authentic people? This is a question of self-honour.

A Question of Honour

The Chinese do not care who loves or hates them. They are building China amidst all the criticism and hatred coming from all corners of the world. They do not need Western affirmation. They have no need or use for it. They love and honour themselves. True, the Chinese have their fair share of domestic problems that include abuse of basic human rights and the absence of democracy.

Contrary to the views of Western leaders, these are their problems to solve, not anyone else's. One thing they can be proud of is that they are not receiving plates of ready-made stew from Europe, America or anywhere else. They own their land. They have built their economy from the ground up. Their language is alive and is now recognised and studied globally. Do you remember when there were talks of South Africans having to learn how to read and write Mandarin? *He he he he he, Thixo wase George Gorch!*

The identity of the Chinese is clear and well understood everywhere in the world. They will never undermine themselves in exchange for acceptance from another race. They will never suck up to another race or nation for their survival. If they should be oppressed, it would be by their leaders and not by another race. Their oppression is a "family matter" to be dealt with amongst themselves. It is none of anyone's business.

A Word of Advice

To further illustrate my point, consider this article written by the renowned author, political analyst, commentator, and influential thinker, Prince Mashele. This politically incorrect piece was published in the October 14, 2014, issue of *The Sowetan* newspaper.

> *Look at us, we show no love and affection for each other, and yet we demand it from white people.*

STUPID AFRICAN, LET YOUR CHILD BE AFRICAN
By Prince Mashele

Twenty–eight years since Ngugi wa Thiong'o wrote his famous book, Decolonizing the Mind, some among the South African black middle class still don't understand the politics of language. There are black parents in our multiracial suburbs and even in townships who speak English to their children, to the extent that the children can neither speak nor understand a single African language. Without realising it, these English - obsessed parents are breeding a bizarre group of unidentifiable people who will be neither black nor white. In years to come, this culturally floating group will be difficult to explain. What kind of black South African would it be who can't speak a single black language?

All South African black parents who speak English to their children don't understand that they, themselves are living examples of the success of white people in relegating African culture. Language is not a neutral conveyor of ideas; it is a culture-laden vehicle. Africans use language to show respect when they address older people. We don't call our older sisters "Nancy" or cousins "Peter". There is a prefix system in the structure of African languages that denotes respect. We say "Sis' Thandi", "Mzala Vusi" or "Bab'uDlamini". When the grannies throw riddles at our children it is a way of embedding culture in children. Thus, the children grow up as part of a distinct culture group in the midst of other cultures.

This is how human life gains the colour-fulness authored by the Creator.

It is politics that teaches Africans to despise their culture, and to be proud of the English language and culture. Nothing in the English language is superior, and indeed nothing in African languages is inferior. What is distorted is the mind of an African parent who teaches his or her child to speak English at the expense of an African language?

We Africans allow our children to be taught English at school simply because global politics has dealt us a blow. The English have vanquished us; they have made us their linguistic appendage.

The process of appendagisation of Africans lead to the situation in which "English was assumed to be the natural language of literature and even political mediation between African people", as Wa Thiong'o observes. But, at the core, this was a political ploy designed by whites to make Africans believe that everything white is superior and everything black is inferior.

White people tried it not only on Africans, but on other nations too. It did not succeed in China, it failed in Japan, and the Italians were hopeless in Ethiopia. Ethiopians are proud of their official language, Amharic, and they don't speak any European languages. They enlist the services of an interpreter when they need to communicate with Europeans, just as the Japanese do. In fact, Japan demonstrated many moons ago that the notion that non-European countries can make scientific progress only by adopting a European language is grossly fallacious.

Learning from Westerners, and using their own languages, the Japanese developed their economy to the extent that until recently, it was the second-largest economy in the world.

Today this second place in the world is occupied not by a European country but by another Asian country that clings tenaciously to its language: China. All this is not to say that Europeans have not contributed ideas to human progress.

Evidence abounds that they have indeed made immense contribution to the development of science and technology. Europeans themselves know and are honest about the fact that their progress in science was in part a culmination of many discoveries made outside

Europe. Indeed, the people who lived outside Europe have made their own discoveries long before they came into contact with Europeans – hence the great civilisations of imperial China, Egypt, Aksum and Mapungubwe, to name a few.

Quite clearly what is known as western science is a universal accumulation of human experience, and thus a truly universal heritage of mankind. Africans should be as proud of western scientific inventions as Europeans cherish the gold and diamonds buried in the African soil. What then, is wrong with the members of the black middle class in South Africa who try very hard to convert their children into little Englishmen? The Bible would say: "Forgive them, for they know not what they do". Such blacks don't understand that astronomy can be studied in a non-European language. The Japanese study astronomy.

These ignorant Africans don't know that there are members of high society in China, truly educated human beings, who drive a Ferrari without speaking a word in Italian, English or French.

So please, dear stupid African parent, allow your child to become African. Leave the task of teaching

> *English to teachers at school, and speak IsiZulu, Sesotho or TshiVenda at home. If you don't understand the politics of languages, please go to Ngugi wa Thiong'o book Decolonising the Mind. You will learn.*

Now, if this does not get you thinking, I will need a special session with you, your parents, your grandparents and all your ancestors. The issues Mashele raises must ignite a mental revolution that seeks to express the colourfulness of our culture and language as designed by our Creator.

Please repeat after me: *I am an African. I am blessed with an African culture and an African language. I love my culture. I love my language. I will continue to explore the beauty of my culture and language for as long as I live, and I will teach my children to do the same.*

> *It is not the lack of money that keeps us under the White man's cultural yoke. It is our lack of pride, vision, passion, cooperation, agreement, commitment and desire to build through sweat and tears. We have a bankruptcy of willpower not money.*

3

ECONOMIC STUPIDITY

"Any time you stop producing and focus only on consuming, you have nothing to be proud of, other than what you consume ... and until we start taking over our communities, understanding our market, and getting our lion's share of the market we will never get up."

Bishop T.D. Jakes

The year 2010 was an important milestone in South Africa. It marked the 150th anniversary of the arrival of Indians in this country. They had been brought over as indentured labourers to work in the sugar plantations of KwaZulu-Natal. They came with nothing except a few personal belongings. I am not a history expert, so I will venture no further.

The Celebration of 150th Anniversary

They celebrated their 150th anniversary knowing that their economic state as Indians living in South Africa was now far better than that of the indigenous people. You would have noticed that by 2010, the Indian business community was already employing hundreds of thousands of Black people across various industries. Can you imagine that? Migrants, who arrived in our country only one hundred and fifty plus years ago as cheap labour are now employers of the indigenous Black people of South Africa and are using them as cheap labour. This shows that while we were fast asleep and accepting the economic status quo, the Indians were busy breaking the White man's yoke from their necks.

Of course, they can speak for themselves on how they managed to improve their general economic position and welfare as a racial group. However, something that dawned on me from early in my observations is that they have radically transformed their position by mastering the prudent and ancient art of circulating money amongst themselves. In most of their communities they own small shopping centres, also known as plazas, which they all support. Indians understand the importance of putting their own interests first. They prioritise, protect and promote those interests through the ancient wisdom that has built every strong economic community in the world – circulating money within national or racial borders. It is strange that despite how ancient this wisdom is, and how evident and universal its results are, Black people still do not practice it. We will never escape the pathetic economic condition our communities are trapped in until we adopt this model

Look at Us

Unlike our communities, the Indian community values itself, its culture and beliefs so much that they will ensure that every rand that comes into their community stays there for as long as possible before it can be allowed to escape. This they do, not only to their benefit and to the continued strengthening of their collective economic muscle, but also to keep their pride and dignity intact. This is nothing new. Economically strong races are those who ensure that once money enters their community, it circulates within it several times before it can be allowed to leave.

Every cent that flows in must add value to their communities several times first before it can be allowed to exit. Whites understand this principle. They have been circulating money amongst themselves for many centuries. Just take a closer look at the Jewish community and you will see why. Despite being a small population and victims of the holocaust, they control a significant chunk of the wealth of the world. They are the gurus of keeping money within their community. They have learnt the ancient secret of circulating money and we must follow suit if we are to change our fortunes.

Our Struggle with the Obvious

We are the only people group who do not think twice before money flows out of our hands into the hands of other racial groups. Money leaves our communities minutes after it comes into our hands. We do not seem to recognise the importance and the value of deliberately and systematically buying from within our racial group. Circulating money amongst ourselves is not just about making economic progress, it is also about keeping our dignity and pride intact.

Self-Affliction

Did you know that our spending patterns as Black people have produced many Indian millionaires? A Stats SA report showed that black people constitute 49,3% of all domestic expenditure. For the same reason, we have also produced many white millionaires and billionaires. However, we have produced very few black millionaires, if any, because our spending patterns are working against us. We are happy to continually create more white millionaires and billionaires while creating no such within our racial group. We have even gone further and created

Chinese and Pakistani millionaires. We seem to be on a roll enriching other races; never thinking about creating Black millionaires. How stupid is that?

It saddens me when I see how of all the racial groups in Mzansi, our race possesses the most potent purchasing power in the land, yet we continually and foolishly misappropriate this power because of our economic stupidity and ignorance.

We do not appreciate that every rand we spend is either strengthening or weakening our economic position as a race. Now considering the purchasing power that we hold we can create thousands of black millionaires within a very short space of time by simply changing our spending patterns. We just need to get our act together and work on an agenda that empowers us and move us higher up the economic ladder. Then again, there is an even bigger problem: we are not aware that we can produce black millionaires. We have concluded, before trying, that the effort is futile. We are so pessimistic about the black man's chances of attaining marketplace success; so much so that we have become sharpshooters of every possible opportunity to elevate a black person. We struggle with the obvious, especially when it comes to enriching our communities by circulating money within our racial borders. It is as if an eternal spell was cast on our minds. *O kare ba re loile. Kwangathi sithakathiwe.*

> *Circulating money amongst ourselves is not just about making economic progress, it is also about keeping our dignity and pride intact.*

Black Solutions to Black Problems

Statistics show that our country has a massive unemployment problem which has been compounded by the COVID-19 pandemic. Both government and private industries are failing to address the acute unemployment rate. Most of the unemployed people in South Africa are black. It can then be deducted that unemployment is the Black man's problem; therefore, the Black man must solve it.

Tragically, we believe jobs must come from White people. Wrong! This notion is foolish! There is enough money flowing out of the hands of Black people that can go a long way towards drastically reducing the high levels of unemployment affecting us as a nation and as black communities. We must start circulating more of the lucrative *"Black rand"* amongst ourselves and it will not be long before we see the radical transformation of our economic position.

We must start supporting each other's businesses and hustles as if our lives depend on it. The money flowing through us is more than enough to generate bountiful empowerment opportunities for our people. The problem is that our money is constantly flowing out of our hands and into the hands of other racial groups who will never plough back into the improvement of the same black communities that continually enrich them. I repeat, that money will never be channelled to the improvement of black communities!

If we loved ourselves enough, we would stop enriching other races at our expense and to our detriment. If we valued ourselves, we would circulate most of our *"Black rand"* within our communities so that our businesses thrive. When the black business community prospers, we are empowered to create jobs for many unemployed members of our communities, particularly youth and women. The challenge of black unemployment lies squarely on our shoulders and it is ours to solve. We must accept this challenge, come together and agree to eradicate unemployment by using the *"Black rand"* within our communities more. Now, before you assume I am promoting the tolerance of black mediocrity, allow me to make this crystal clear.

#BlackMediocrityMustFall

As we develop and master the practice of circulating money amongst ourselves, we must demand nothing short of excellence and a strong work ethic from one another. We must challenge each other to keep improving the quality of our products and services as we support each other. We should stretch each other to develop innovative products and services that will serve the needs of our communities adequately. Let us engage one another, open doors for one another, and create more and more opportunities to uplift our own. Let us start here and now, and we will get there, slowly but surely. Let us do it for the sake of our black pride, our future and our race. Let us do it, black man! I know we can do this!

> *As we develop and master the practice of circulating money amongst ourselves, we must demand nothing short of excellence and a strong work ethic from one another.*

When Economic Power Meets Economic Stupidity

Allow me to illustrate the massive power we have as a people. Are you aware that if we, the so-called poor and previously disadvantaged black majority, would stop buying from all major supermarkets and mega-retailers, they would collapse within six months? **Yebo yes!** That is how much economic power lies in our hands as the "previously disadvantaged" and "poor black" people of South Africa. Let us say this slowly so we can reflect upon it and understand it:

If we, the so-called poor and the previously disadvantaged black majority, would stop buying from all grocery and clothing chain stores, the

Pakistani spazas, and the Indian plazas in South Africa, all these businesses would collapse within six months or less.

Do you see the power you hold? Do you realise what this collective power we possess can achieve? As mentioned before, we account for about half of all consumption in South Africa, while Whites, Indians, and other races share the other half. There you have it, Black man, we hold economic power in Mzansi. As incredible, heart-warming and empowering as that may sound, we can only benefit from this economic power when we come together as one and begin to channel our **"Black rand"** back into our communities and circulating as much of it there for as long as possible.

The Crux of It

Our rand must work for our race and our communities more than it does for others. It must serve our interests and not those of white monopoly capitalists as it has always done and continues to do.

Whenever you use your *"Black rand"* to buy from other racial groups, Whites, Indians, Jews, Chinese, and Pakistanis, you are empowering them to become stronger than yourself economically. *Mncwi Struu, Ungizwe.* Hear me well – you are empowering them to become better, stronger and more powerful than yourself. Whenever you act this stupidly, you are implying that it is okay for Blacks to stay in shacks, four-roomed houses and in highly concentrated and densely populated townships while the people you empower with your rand use the money to live lavishly in the luxurious estates of the likes of Houghton, Silverlakes, Bantry Bay and Mount Edgecombe.

You are taking the bread you should be feeding your starving children with and giving it to their unappreciative children, whose stomachs are already overflowing. You are keeping their children and relatives employed while you, your children, and their cousins loiter around the streets, drowning in the despair of unemployment. No wonder Black children easily fall prey to drug dealers and human traffickers.

Each time you buy from other races, you are foolishly empowering them to go and stay in grand residential areas, drive luxury cars and ensure job security for their own, while you experience the direct opposite.

You are giving them the ammunition to continually exclude and enslave us economically.

> *Our rand must work for our race and our communities more than it does for others.*

The Gini Coefficient

The Gini coefficient is a measure of economic inequality. It reflects the distribution of wealth within a nation. Now, if you suffer from any chronic condition please ensure that you take your medication before you proceed reading this book. The following information is so painful that it could exacerbate your condition.

South Africa has the highest Gini coefficient in the whole world. In case you missed it the first time allow me to repeat myself, South Africa has the highest Gini coefficient in the whole world. Simply put, it means the minority (Whites) controls most of the wealth in the country while the majority

(Blacks) are forced to share the remaining meagre crumbs. Using the Pareto 80/20 principle, it means that 20% of the people (Whites) own 80% of the country's wealth, while 80% of the population (Blacks) are scrambling for the remaining 20% of the wealth. This therefore means, if you are Black like me, you have played a huge role in empowering the minority Whites to enjoy 80% of the nation's wealth through your ignorant and thoughtless spending patterns.

Lalela

Lalela muntu omnyama. Listen, Black man. How can you be so cruel, heartless and dangerous towards yourself? Wake up, Black man, wake up! ***Vuka!*** Look at you! You are ever giving Whites, Indians, Chinese, Jews and Pakistanis power, convenience, comfort and luxury at the expense of your interests, economic well-being, and your children's future. We are giving them all this because we do not circulate money amongst ourselves. For as long as we continue to despise one another and refuse to support each other, this will be our plight forever. Look at us! So powerful yet so stupid.

You and I, Black man, are a sad story to tell. *Eish*, a very sad story indeed. We have such an endearment towards the plates of ready-made stew every racial group is offering us. We are foolishly channelling our economic muscle to the betterment of others and our continued demise and detriment. How stupid is that? **Cabanga nje! Nagana fela!**

Food for Thought

The Start of the Revolution

If Black people in South Africa would stop buying from all the major chain supermarkets, service providers, clothing shops and furniture stores in the country, these conglomerates would not survive. No other racial group in South Africa possesses that kind of power, not even one. We are the only ones who have the power to frustrate the economy by holding back and redirecting our buying power. I repeat, no other racial group in South Africa possesses our measure of power. That is what we mean by **black power.**

Amandla! Matla!

- *Whites do not possess this power.*
- *Indians do not possess this power.*

- *Chinese do not possess this power.*
- *Pakistanis do not possess this power.*
- *Only Black people have this power.* **Thina sodwa!**

If we would start by spending just 30% of our disposable income amongst ourselves, we would make a huge and significant difference in the quality of the lives of the black majority in townships.

Sadly, we never harness this power to our advantage and progress; instead, we keep giving it away, recklessly so. We are a powerful people who keep giving their power away to powerless people. *We are making the powerless powerful while we the powerful become more and more powerless as we are forced to scramble for the meagre crumbs that fall from the tables of the powerless people we have made powerful.*

Driving the Nail In

If PEP, Edgars, Jet, Shoprite, Pick n' Pay, Ellerines, Morkels, Spar etc. can thrive and become massive businesses with multi-billion-rand worth of market capitalisation propelled by the stupidity our spending habits and patterns suggest, imagine what would happen if we changed. Strangely, the truth eludes us. We do not even see that we are a super economic force. We are, in fact, the mainstream of the economy but we just do not know this. We have no understanding of our power.

> *Look at us, so powerful and yet so stupid.*

A Light at the End of the Tunnel

The good news is that the economic challenges that affect us are not insurmountable. These are resolvable issues. We are just ignorant and have not been applying our minds, wisdom, insight, understanding and energy towards their resolution. Maybe we were genuinely and sincerely ignorant about this all along, but the days of ignoring such destructive habits must end. Time to rise Black man and break this yoke of economic stupidity and foolishness! It is time we turned the tables around. It is time we reclaimed what is rightfully ours in our land. No more self-destruction and self-defeat. Rise, oh Black man, rise! *Phambili! Asijiki!* Can I get an amen right here?

Failure to understand the power of circulating money amongst ourselves has thrown us into a dark, poverty-stricken and hopeless dungeon. For some of us, our children and grandchildren were born, and raised in this dungeon. But should they die in it? Black man is that really what you want? I mean, really? There will be no end in sight for the powerful but poor Black man who ignores the wisdom of money circulation within his own race.

The Root of the Problem

"A kingdom divided against itself cannot stand."

Jesus Christ

So, why are we economically marginalised and dwelling on the periphery when we possess enormous economic power? Simply put, we are divided by our despise for each other based on idiotic stereotypes. As a result, we struggle to come together to bring down this Goliath of economic stupidity, who stands and mocks us daily. Failing to unite has relegated us and our posterity to languish at the side lines of the economy, where, like poor Lazarus in the Bible, we wait for peanuts and crumbs that fall from the White master's table.

Sesfikile: A Case in Point

South Africa has a huge and thriving black-dominated taxi industry. Research has shown that over 70% of South Africans use taxis, of which the most users are blacks. According to a report published by Transaction Capital in 2019, South Africa's taxi industry recorded over R50 billion in turnover in the year 2018 – a clear sign of our massive economic power as Black people.

The taxi associations across the country possesses the economic muscle to build a huge business empire if they were more united in their business endeavours. Their massive, consolidated power would capacitate and catapult them to make inroads into any industry that is connected to their core business.

A simple example is the petroleum sector. The local taxi industry and its associations could easily build or buy franchises and own their filling stations across the entire country if they chose to.

The taxis they operate and other vehicles would fill up at these stations, and they could even grow to take greater control of the petroleum industry. With over 250 000 taxis operating across the country, the taxi industry could build a 100% black-owned business empire to be reckoned with.

They can set up their own financial institutions and provide funeral cover for their members and users if they could leverage this economic power. However, here we are once again, blind to our power and ignorant of the massive opportunities at our disposal. We would rather fight over petty issues than unite for our own good. The opportunities are endless. A brainstorming session on the issue could reveal a vast lineup of the ocean of opportunities that can be explored.

Economically Ambushed

Allow me to cast the net wider and illustrate how our economic power is being used to stifle us and keep us subjugated as a race. We have been seeing the mushrooming of shopping malls being built by white developers in black townships across the country. These developers approach municipalities to purchase vacant land for the erection of these malls. The municipalities, who are desperate for income and revenue, quickly agree to sell these empty spaces to the white-owned developers. The developers then approach banks and retailers to come on board and make their dream of these township shopping malls come true.

Few, if any, of these entities (the developers, banks and retailers) are owned by Black people; therefore, none of them exists to promote black interests even though they are on black residential soil. The mega-retailers, who are ever looking to expand their market share within that Living Standards Measure (LSM), are quick to sign permanent lease agreements with these malls to keep their competitors at bay. The banks also agree to invest in the development of these malls; they too sign permanent lease agreements with the developers.

All these players come together and work efficiently to target one big fat and stupid cash cow, the black consumer. A mall is then established in a township with little of that development, if any, going towards the empowerment of Black people. The only exception is that of the King Pie franchise and the few fortunate labourers who will be employed by the giant retail outlets. Otherwise, it is all lily white.

> *We are the only race with the power to shut down all the major supermarkets, service providers, clothing shops, and furniture stores in the country.*

When local small black-owned businesses try to get into these malls, they are tactically excluded by the complex lease agreements and exorbitant rentals which only the "white boys" can afford. So, what happens? Very few, if any, black-owned businesses enter this lucrative economic space. As for the small shopping complexes in the township that are black-owned, they struggle to compete and slowly die, never to rise again. They are not necessarily killed by these shopping malls but killed by the gullibility of black consumers.

How we conveniently forget that during the dark economic days of apartheid these black township entrepreneurs, though they were also battered by apartheid, stood by us and brought within our reach daily household necessities.

The Sad Reality

What is saddest about this is how we are happy coming in as cheap labour and as consumers who fill up all the supermarkets, clothing stores, and furniture retailers because we do not see what is taking place in the bigger picture and scheme of things. To the undiscerning black eye, these malls look like upgrades to our communities and conveniences designed to improve our lives; contrarywise, they are funnels created to siphon more of the lucrative *"Black rand"* out of our communities and channel it back into the hands of white monopoly capitalists.

A plate of ready-made stew is being exchanged for a birthright blessing right here. We get a mall in exchange for the power we could use to build our race and communities.

When the malls open, the white monopoly capitalists pop expensive bottles of Champagne in their Sandton boardrooms, celebrating another easy victory over this ignorant fat cash cow called the Black man. They have secured business for generations; Christmas has come early for them once again, and it is party time. As for us, our struggle not only continues but deepens. Black man you need to get restless about this or else you will perpetuate the pathetic disposition of being a means to an end for all other races. *Selah!* – pause and reflect.

> *We are making the powerless powerful, and we the powerful become more and more powerless as we are forced to scramble for the meagre crumbs that fall from the tables of the powerless people who we have made powerful.*

My Own Experiences

I usually go to Soshanguve Crossing – a new mall close to where I live – to watch the crazy activity that dominates the mall every single month-end. Black people jam-pack the mall to the point where everyone struggles to move comfortably. All the retail shops would be packed beyond capacity. You will see Black people walk out of the mall with overflowing trolleys. This picture makes me think, are we not like sheep that blindly go to the slaughter to voluntarily give away our economic vitality gained from our blood, sweat and tears? Are we not naively giving away our lucrative *"Black rand"* to the very same oppressive masters of our past? *Selah!*

What is even more disheartening is that out of all this foolish excitement, chaotic mayhem and hive of activity, few Black people, if any, are benefitting.

No one forces us to spend money on other races. It is something we passionately love and enjoy. We happily volunteer to be economic slaves of all other races. We seem to derive a sense of importance and significance from being seen carrying loaded plastics from major retailers. We wear foreign brands and brag to our friends and relatives about living the high life. *Nigga,* please!

We are nothing more than voluntary slaves, who are too lazy to liberate themselves by burning their own pot of stew. We have settled for enjoying the bonds of economic oppression and slavery. **Hayi, kunzima. Lafa elihle kakhulu!**

Please take some time to stand at your nearest black township shopping mall at the end of the month, Black Friday or festive season. See the throngs of Black people flooding these malls; you would not even find parking space. Watch as we exit the mall with trolleys overflowing with food, alcohol, clothing and appliances. Imagine the rand value of these transactions as you see Black people leaving the mall. Please help me answer this pertinent question, who is the ultimate benefactor out of all this economic activity? Who is being empowered in all these transactions? Is it the marginalised Blacks or the capitalist Whites?

> *...are we not like sheep that blindly go to the slaughter to voluntarily give away their economic vitality, gained from their blood, sweat, and tears?*

The Power of One

If unity was our strength and circulating money amongst ourselves was common practice, we would collectively lobby against municipalities selling vacant lands in our communities to white developers without consulting us as primary stakeholders. We would promote and protect our interests more effectively and ensure that they are not compromised in any way. This is what the Jewish and Indian people would undoubtedly do if such activities were to happen in their communities.

We must learn from the Jewish and come together to devise a detailed plan of engagement that ensures black businesses are adequately represented in these massive developments. To achieve this, we need to first attain unity of purpose, vision and direction. We cannot afford to be divided any longer.

Division weakens us but unity will give us all the power we need to lobby for a fat share of the pie. Through unity we can lay down all the necessary terms and conditions that will ensure tangible, sustainable and undeniable benefit of the black community in these developments. We can ensure that our people are prioritised when contracts are awarded, they are prioritised for business finance, they are prioritised in direct corporate social investments, and supported to acquire retail space and franchises. We can insist on ensuring that we too are actively involved at all levels – from conception, ownership, development, management and operation of these shopping malls. We can ensure that this development works for us and not against us. This is what people who are conscious of their power do. If only we were united.

Desperate Times, Desperate Measures

Any form of township developments should primarily benefit the community within that township.

For something of this magnitude to be achieved, a strong united community that has fortitude, zeal, focus, knowledge, understanding, wisdom, self-respect and willpower is needed. This kind of unity must start at the grassroots level of our communities. We can work with our existing community structures and through them mobilise ourselves to approach our municipalities with a sound and solid business case and challenge them with the aim of turning the tide to the black community's advantage. *Asijiki!*

As Black people, the attributes of unity, common purpose and will-power seem to evade us.

Hence, we do not raise our voices in discontent when these malls are erected right under our noses without us having a say. In our eyes, we see these as community upgrades. We have this tendency of feeling included in the elite class when Checkers, Woolworths, Ster Kinekor, McDonald's, Spur, and the many other *"superior"* retail outlets set-up-shop in our communities. Black man, learn to evaluate the true opportunity cost of these malls and refuse to senselessly support these entities that continually impoverish our race. The same applies when big trans-national mining houses come to set up a mine in our rural communities. Let us not be quick to celebrate our self-betrayal by allowing deals that leave us worse off than before. We must cultivate a new way of interpreting these events. These are not upgrades but indications that you and I are seen as big, fat, humungous and ignorant cash cows by other opportunistic races. And this is on us because like Esau, we love ready-made stew.

The True Cost of a Mall

As alluded to earlier, I am a proud resident of Soshanguve, where a once-thriving shopping complex called Takalani was located – in Block L Section. It was an inspiring model of excellent black township entrepreneurship. This complex, together with many others in the community, was brought down to its knees by the establishment of Soshanguve Crossing. Currently, there are very few, if any, black-owned general dealers in my township that feed off the *"Black rand"* circulating in the community, because it is all flowing out to other races. The remnants are the few black enterprises that survive from running shebeens/taverns, hair salons, vegetable vendors and, selling *Sphatlho/Kota* (township burger). Other than these lucky few, there is nothing. *Dololo!*

I guess one day, we will look at many such businesses in our townships and say, "Rest in peace black township entrepreneurs. Thank you for going all out and standing by us during the dark apartheid era. Now that we have achieved democracy, we have sold you out in favour of the plate of ready-made stew from white monopoly capitalists. You have fallen because we betrayed you and now you can either go and find a job in one of the retail outlets at Soshanguve Crossing or starve to death."

Shall we bow our heads and observe a moment of silence for the businesses we have destroyed because of our stupidity.

Morena boloka setjhaba sa heso!

Selah!

Our Self-Inflicted Poverty

We are suffering from self-inflicted poverty because we have allowed ourselves to be a fat cash cow for the entire world. I wonder how the whole world realised that Black people are so economically gullible that they are willing to see black businesses die a slow death while injecting vitality and steroids into the businesses of other races.

What is the Bait?

It is as though when a Pakistani, a Chinese, an Arab or a businessman from anywhere in the world feels ripe and ready for business, they quickly set sail to a black township in South Africa. I can imagine the conversation used as bait:

Rasheed, come to South Africa there is a huge, fat, illustrious and unsuspecting cash cow here. You will have no resistance here. They will help you establish your business at the expense of their very own. That is how defenceless and naïve they are. They will lease their spaza shops to you and settle for a meagre rental because they are too lazy to cook their own stew. My friend rather than sit and be frustrated by life in Pakistan, come to South Africa. Here you will thrive. There is a lot of easy money to be made.

Their borders are porous, and their Home Affairs department is useless and corrupt. Move quickly before their eyes open and secure for yourself a desperate woman who will marry you for R5000 in exchange for residency. You do not have to live with her, it is a purely transactional relationship. From there you are set for life. Soon you will be employing these gullible blacks in your business.

They all think the same way. They are easy to manipulate and squeeze. They have no clue of how powerful they are. Even if you go to their poorest communities, you will still do better than survive.

Now, my Black brothers and sisters please tell me, is this how you would love to continue to be perceived?

- *Do you want the next ten generations of children who come from your loins to be perceived as such?*
- *Is this the legacy you want to leave?*
- *When are you going to stand up to promote your interests?*
- *Will you ever decide to put yourself first?*
- *Will you ever learn to stop and think about the severe consequences of your actions and foolishness?*
- *Are you so stupid and naïve that you do not have time to think before you act?*

Please think about this, reflect on it and begin to change the way you do things because you are setting your children up for economic disaster in favour of the instant gratification you derive from ready-made stews.

I can sense that this is making you teary but hang tight and stay put for the truth will set you free.

Unalarmed

Despite the overwhelming evidence that is before us, we do not seem to be alarmed by the utter stupidity that we continue to display, as we show no signs of a people attempting to correct their flaws. Our attitudes, behaviours and conversations do not reflect a people looking forward to a day when the world will be consuming the products we produce. All we ever do is consume, consume and consume.

We do not show any engrossed intention to play in the big league of the mainstream economy. That being the case, what kind of entrepreneurship, leadership and business acumen do we hope to develop for future generations?

We happily choose to support other nations and racial groups to our detriment and demise. By just mastering the wisdom and the power of circulating money and doing business amongst ourselves, we can significantly reduce the impact apartheid, poverty, inequality and marginalisation on our communities. That is exactly what the Indians have managed to achieve in the one hundred and fifty plus years that they been here.

That is why they are not suffering from the aftereffects of apartheid like we are. *Rona e re gobaditse. Rona re latlhlile. Because ons is moegoes!* We are clueless!

"The greatest tragedy in life is not death, but a life without purpose"

Dr Myles Munroe

"The only thing worse than being blind is having sight but no vision."

Helen Keller

The Indian Economic Revolution

Have you ever taken a moment to study the shopping culture of the Indians in South Africa and around the world? If you have never done so, allow me to let you in on their secret.

- *You hardly ever see Indians pushing a grocery trolley in Shoprite or Pick n' Pay, or buying*

- *clothes at Edgars, Truworths and/or Mr. Price? Open your eyes and see for yourself.*
- *It is not often that you see an Indian standing in a queue at a Standard Bank or Absa Bank. I dare you.*
- *You hardly ever see Indians carrying big plastic bags from a shopping spree in these rand sucking parasitic shopping malls. Check it out.*

Does this mean that Indians do not eat, dress or bank? They do! They intentionally, deliberately and wisely ensure the following:

- *Indian money circulates within their communities and they work hard to ensure that most of it remains there.*
- *Like the Jews and the Afrikaners, Indians appreciate that circulating money within their community is the most effective way to build wealth and rise economically. In this way, they create their own economy within the main economy that would go a long way in sustaining them should things go sour.*

My Observation

A while ago I spent some time in the mainstream retail outlets of Durban; just watching and making visual observations and mental notes. Remember, Durban is the city with the highest population of Indians within South Africa. During my observation, I noticed that Indians generally do not buy groceries or clothes from these leading chain stores. They work there but you rarely ever see them in their numbers buying from these places as you would Black and White people. Indians are so loyal to their culture and cuisine; they hardly ever patron mainstream restaurants and fast-food outlets. They buy from Indian takeaways in plazas within their communities. They buy clothes, phones, groceries and accessories from each other and never from any other race. I challenge you to verify my submission by making your observations. My Black brothers and sisters out there in Durban, please feel free to let me know. Ping me at info@sakhilesibiya.co.za.

Malls will Never Survive in Indian Communities

Have you ever noticed that these shopping malls, which are mushrooming in black townships are never established in residential communities that are predominantly Indian? There are no such malls in places like Laudium in Pretoria and other communities with a sizeable Indian population. I have never seen a Shoprite, Pick n Pay, Edgars or an Ellerines outlet in Indian communities.

You may be wondering why? This is what I think:

- *Indians have learned the secret of circulating money within their racial group and they have been doing it for centuries.*
- *Indians have deliberately, purposely and intentionally resolved in their hearts that if they need to purchase anything, they will exhaust every possibility of buying it from their fellow Indians before painfully considering going to spend their money on other races. Even then, it will not be long before they identify and address the gap as a business opportunity within their community that needs to be taken advantage of by one of them and supported by all of them. Selah!*
- *Indians have mastered the art of selling to different racial groups while only buying from their own, and truth be told, they are very good at it.*

Imagine how far we would go as Black people if we began channelling 30% of our disposable income into supporting black-owned businesses. Imagine where we would be ten, twenty, fifty and a hundred and fifty years from now. It is inconceivable. ***Yhooo!*** Massive!

Indians have realised that as a race, they do not need to be served plates of ready-made stew by other races because it reduces them to a bunch of nobodies. They only buy from their kind and by so doing they have empowered their race to become the economic giants they are today. Apartheid has had a much lesser impact on them than it has had on Black people because they have mastered this art. That is why they are far ahead of Black people economically. They are even doing better than some White people. They have managed to create their own economy, and continue efforts to defend, sustain and grow it.

They do not have the numbers to make their economy strong and agile, but they have positioned themselves to draw mainly from the gigantic purchasing power of Black people. Yes, we are the unsuspecting and ignorant cash cow that they milk.

The Indians have become so good at milking other races that they have already started tapping into the buying power of Whites as well. With the support of the "Indian rand" the "White rand", and the massive *"Black rand"*, the Indian community is well on their way to economic paradise. If they did it, surely, we can *did it* too.

Pakistani Invasion

Our black townships have also been invaded by a tsunami of spaza shops operated by Pakistanis. Pakistani migration to South Africa does not date back one hundred and fifty years as is the case with Indian migration. It is however clear that they are also aware of the power of this unsuspecting, innocent, ignorant and gullible Black man regardless of how educated, enlightened and sophisticated he may appear to be – the very same Black man who has created countless White and Indian millionaires and billionaires. They know that they can also cash in on this fast asleep, naïve, fat and lazy-to-think cash cow by simply setting up spaza shops in their communities. They have also become aware that we are such lovers of convenience and ease that we will gladly betray our souls and destinies in exchange for these pleasures of comfort.

Sell Outs

When the Pakistanis started their migration into South Africa, Black people were running all the spaza shops in the townships. I guess what shocked the Pakistanis – almost to the point of wetting their pants – was that we were willing to surrender our spaza industry to them without resistance, in exchange for chicken feed. Guess what the Pakistanis did? *They called all their buddies, from far and wide, telling them that they have found a land flowing with milk and honey, whose inhabitants saw themselves as grasshoppers and nothing more.* So, they began to move into South Africa with a drive to remorselessly milk this naïve and gullible cash cow – the Black man.

Just imagine if the Black people owning spaza shops were as united as the taxi owners' associations. They would protect their industry with everything they have and everybody, including government, would know that the spaza industry is a no-go zone.

Just like you wouldn't make decisions that will impact the taxi industry negatively without facing major resistance from them, the same should have occurred with the spaza industry. They should have organised themselves into a formidable forum where nothing about them is done or discussed without them. Everybody would have trodden carefully and cautiously when it comes to the spaza territories. The good news though is that it is not too late to consider setting up such a forum. The spaza industry should unapologetically and unashamedly be reclaimed by the Black man. Who is ready to go first?

> *We are such lovers of convenience and ease that we will gladly betray our souls and destinies in exchange for these pleasures of comfort.*

Our Stokvel Mentality

Just as we can come together as Black people and organise ourselves into stokvels for funerals and distributing groceries at the end of the year, we can, in the same way, mobilise ourselves and reclaim our spaza industry. I have a friend who works for a company that uses the spaza industry as a major distribution channel for its products. He told me that the spaza industry is a billion-rand industry. It is an industry which could have been benefitting Blacks if we were not so ignorant.

A Predator's Game

Whenever the Pakistanis see Black people, they see an opportunity; the same way a ravenous wolf sees a hearty meal when it sees a naïve and weak prey. A predator drools at the thought of digging its thirsty teeth into a fattened and naïve cash cow. The Pakistanis are careful to study the patterns and weaknesses of Black people just as the wolf does its prey. Our undiscerning nature and lack of shrewdness expose us to their craftiness, in the same way that Esau's stupidity made him an unsuspecting target and victim of Jacob.

The Pakistanis have been able to figure us out just as the White man, the Chinese and the Indian have figured us out. We are such a simple-minded people that sucking the **"Black rand"** out of our communities is easier than taking candy from a baby. For this reason, you'd find Pakistanis in our rural areas, cities, shopping malls, and in black townships.

What contributes to their success is also that they are a united front. They use their numbers to buy their products in bulk at huge discounts. They boast collaborative skills of par excellence. Through their unity, they order huge quantities directly from the manufacturers and match (at times undercut) the prices of conglomerate chain stores.

The Pakistanis have even gone as far as investing in warehouses where they store large quantities of stock to distribute to their own at extremely competitive prices. Even as we speak, the Pakistani front is seen as the major distribution channel for many products that see their way into the townships, where the majority of Black South Africans live. Sometimes I really wonder whether we as Black people are just breathing or we are living.

The Pakistanis began by putting their foot in the door, now they have pushed the door wide open for themselves. And I promise you that within the next few years, they will be employing the very unsuspecting, ignorant and naïve cash cows that catapulted them into economic progress. They are not playing games. They are ruthless and they mean serious business!

Our Recourse

We need to indoctrinate Black people into the group buying business model. Unity must be our way of thinking and our way of doing business. We cannot be a united front only when we are burying each other, buying groceries together, and distributing cash at the end of the year via socials. The stokvel industry, yes that is what it is now – an industry – is worth billions of rands which we entrust to white-owned financial institutions. Institutions, which will make more money from our money than we Blacks do. What Scripture says is indeed true, *"... people perish for a lack of knowledge."*

> *We need to indoctrinate Black people into the group buying business model. Unity must be our way of thinking and our way of doing business.*

A Finer Analysis

Let us bring this closer to home and ask ourselves the following questions:

- *How many white millionaires have been created by the "Black rand"? **Wololo!** Galore!*
- *How many Indian millionaires have been created by the "Black rand"? **Wololo!** Galore!*
- *How many black millionaires have been created by the "Black rand"? **Dololo!** None!*
- *Are there perhaps any white billionaires created by the "Black rand"? **Wololo, wololo, wololo!** Galore! Galore! Galore!*

Sad, but true, our hard-earned money flees our communities as soon as it flows into it. It has no time to create millionaires in our communities.

With the scenario below, I would like to paint a vivid picture of how the hard-earned cash of a Black man leaves his community to serve and enrich other races.

Mr. Masanabo is from Tembisa and earns a take-home salary of R10 000 a month. It is the 31st of the month and this is generally how his money will be spent over the next 48 hours:

EXPENDITURE	COST	RACE
Fast Food	R 150	White Business
Insurance Policies	R 600	White Business
Bond Repayment	R2 000	White Bank
Groceries	R1 500	White Supermarket
Car Instalment	R1 050	White Financier
Clothing Account	R 500	White Business
Credit Cards and Other Loans	R 700	White Institution
School Fees	R 600	Probably White School
Petrol on Pay Day	R1 000	Probably White Filling Station
Miscellaneous	R 450	Pakistani Spaza Shop
Balance	R1450	Hopefully Black but most likely Pakistani

As you can see, most of the money in the above example went into white businesses within 48 hours of Masanabo receiving his salary, in most cases, in less than hours after the salary reached his bank account. He is left with R1 450 from which R1 000 would be used for fuel to travel to and from work for the whole month. To give him credit, let us believe that he filled his car from a black-owned filling station in the township. But you and I know that the highest probability is that he filled his car from a white-owned petroleum station – I have discovered that most filling stations in black townships are owned by Whites and Indians. The remaining R450 would be petty cash left to buy bread and milk from the nearby spaza, owned by a Pakistani. This is how we as Black people generally spend our money and create millionaires of other races daily.

Just imagine the ripple effect of this behaviour carried out by over 46 million Black people daily. It is huge and mind-boggling. It is almost inconceivable that it results in the enrichment of many Indian, Pakistani, Chinese and White people, and the continued impoverishment of the black masses. This is sad. Extremely sad.

Do yourself a favour and use the table below to chart how much of your money goes into the hands of other races within the first 48 hours of your salary being deposited into your bank account.

EXPENDITURES	COST	RACE
Groceries		
Insurance Policies		
Transport		
Clothing Account		
School Fees		
Rent		
Credit Cards and Other Loans		
Entertainment		
Miscellaneous		
Balance		

Sobering Thoughts

May I kindly request that you close this book for the next thirty minutes, close your eyes and imagine the widespread impact of our foolish behaviour that leaves us in shameful destitution – I am referring to our foolishness of enriching other races through our day-to-day ill-informed spending patterns.

You, the reader, have been doing this for decades. You followed your parents' and grandparents' footsteps, and your children will probably follow you into this madness. Please, please, please! *Asseblief tog! Ngiyacela! Ke a kgopela!* Let this crap stop with you. May you be the one who pulls the handbrake on such stupidity! You shall not pass this self-defeating outrageous madness onto your children! Your children deserve much better than this! Do you hear me? *Uyangizwa? A o a nkutloa?? Virstan jy? Mampara!*

The Sad Reality of Our Economic Clout

The South African economy is fuelled by the sweat and cash power of the black majority. Even though we may not fully understand this, it is the blatant truth. As I said before, if for only one month all Black people in South Africa decided to spend 30% of their disposable income on black-owned businesses, all these white-owned mainstream retailers and other business industries would take a serious knock and black business will experience a major boom. If this broad-based mass action continued for six more months, *it would be the beginning of the long awaited black economic revolution.*

If the spending ratio of Black people on black businesses were to increase to 50% or more, that would be the beginning of the end of these mega retailers and chain stores and the emergence of true black economic emancipation – the kind our ancestors and descendants will honour us for.

No other racial group in South Africa can claim our massive economic power. I will repeat this several times so that it gets through your thick colonised and subdued skulls.

- *No other racial group in South Africa can claim such massive economic power except Black people!*
- *No other racial group in South Africa can claim such massive economic power except Black people!*
- *No other racial group in South Africa can claim such massive economic power except Black people!*
- *No other racial group in South Africa can claim such massive economic power except Black people!*
- *No other racial group in South Africa can claim such massive economic power except Black people!*

- *No other racial group in South Africa can claim such massive economic power except Black people!*
- *No other racial group in South Africa can claim such massive economic power except Black people!*
- *No other racial group in South Africa can claim such massive economic power except Black people!*
- *No other racial group in South Africa can claim such massive economic power except Black people!*
- *No other racial group in South Africa can claim such massive economic power except Black people!*

If you cheated on reading the above sentences word by word, please go back and start afresh. It is essential for shifting your mindset. I am not joking, Black man. I am serious now. Do it for your own good and that of your posterity, and fellow Black brothers and sisters. Stop playing games. I am watching you.

Sadly, those of us who wield such significant economic power, use it to disempower ourselves without even thinking twice.

Awakening the Economic Powerhouse

We have established that Indians buy only from other Indians. Also, we now know that if we remove black consumers from the equation, the support mainstream retailers get from other racial groups, mainly Whites and Coloureds, would not even be enough to cover their basic operational costs. So now, what would happen if we redirected our support to black businesses? I assure you, without delays, black businesses would grow exponentially.

The Cat Is Out of the Bag

The White man and all other racial groups have been hoping for centuries that we would never wake up to this truth. Now that we have uncovered this precious key to true economic liberation and empowerment, I pray that we use it to change our destiny. I am convinced that the White people reading this book are probably sweating profusely as they read this portion. They are hoping that the saying will prove true that *"If you want to hide something from a Black man, put it in a book because he won't read it."* However, I am sorry to announce to you my former White oppressors, we are now *"woke!"* We have become so restless that we are writing books like this one so that the current generations and those yet to come can find the truth that will set them free. We are so determined to break your yoke of domination upon us that we will stop at nothing until we succeed. So, from now on, beware of the Black man! *Swart gevaar!"*

We must awaken this black giant from his deep sleep to the enormous power that lies within him. As the veil of stupidity and ignorance lifts from our eyes, let us rise and stand united as a people who are determined to reclaim their economic nuclear power and might, by channelling our money back into our communities as much as possible.

Let's hold an emergency *indaba* now to reclaim our lost pride, heritage and *"Black rand"*. We will talk more about this *indaba* in the closing chapter.

The Chowing Exercise

From the analysis of Mr Masanabo's spending pattens above, we can conclude that Black people are economically chowed by every race they interact with.

- *Whites chow Blacks!*
- *Indians chow Blacks!*
- *Chinese chow Blacks!*

- *Jews chow Blacks!*
- *Pakistanis chow Blacks!*
- *Whites chow Whites!*
- *Indians chow Indians!*
- *Chinese chow Chinese*
- *Jews chow Jews!*
- *Pakistanis chow Pakistanis!*
- *Blacks don't chow Whites!*
- *Blacks don't chow Indians!*
- *Blacks don't chow Chinese!*
- *Blacks don't chow Jews!*
- *Blacks don't chow Pakistanis!*
- *Even worse, Blacks don't chow Blacks!*
- *Blacks don't chow!*
- *Blacks don't chow fokol!*

No wonder we are weak, poor and hungry; we do not chow anybody. The undeniable evidence is in that for centuries Black people have remained the poorest of all races.

When you chow, you feed yourself and become strong and healthy. But because we Blacks don't chow anybody including our own, we go around hungry. We are ever on the receiving end. Blacks have failed to understand the simplest and most rudimentary law of the jungle which is **chow or be chowed.**

Ge o saje, o tla jewa!

Mawungadli uzodliwa!

Chow or be chowed!

Aren't you tired of being chowed? I mean seriously! *Ngamanye amazwi, sidliwa yizo zonke lezizwe. Abekho esibadlayo, ngisho nangokwethu asidlani kwanhlobo. Kusho khona ukuthi umsebenzi wethu thina bomdabu ukudliwa nje qha! Re a jewa!*

We blacks live to be chowed.

Please tell me how it feels being chowed by everyone while you chow no one.

Poke the Black person sitting next to you and say, *"Uyadliwa wena, wa jewa."*

Also, ask the next Black person you meet:

"Mara kumnandi ukudliwa?"

"Mara go monate go jewa?"

"Awukhathali ukudliwa?"

"Ga o lapise ke go jewa?"

"Uyodliwa kuze kube nini?"

"O jewa go fitlha neng?"

Now to the first White person you meet after this, audibly or silently tell them, *"Your days of chowing me are numbered, you have chowed me enough. I am tired of it. Enough is enough."*

A ke re lapisiweng ke go jewa tog rona bana ba thari e ntsho! Kanti unjani wena uloku udliwa kwangathi uyidombolo?"

#AngisazodliwaNjengeDombolo

#AngisazodliwaOkareKeSphatlo

#IAmDoneWithBeingChowed

> *Blacks have failed to understand the simplest and most rudimentary law of the jungle which is chow or be chowed.*

For the Why?

I came across the following post on one of the social media platforms. Though the source is unknown, it made me think deeply about how much of this could be true. I encourage you to do the same. Instead of becoming defensive, be brutally and ruthlessly honest with yourself Black man, and ask how much of it could be true.

> **Interviewer:** *Why are blacks so behind economically?*
>
> **Jewish leader:** *The only thing blacks understand is consumption. Blacks do not understand the importance of creating and building wealth.*
>
> *The fundamental rule is to keep your money within your racial group. We, the Jews, build Jewish businesses, hire Jewish, buy Jewish and spend Jewish. There is nothing wrong with that, but it is a basic rule, which blacks cannot comprehend and follow. "He kills his fellow blacks daily instead of wanting to see his fellow blacks succeed". 93% of blacks killed in America are killed by other blacks. (And yet we are the ones who shout "Blacks Lives Matter")*

Their leaders steal from their people and send the money back to their colonial masters, from who they borrow the same money.

Every successful black person wants to spend his money in the country of his colonial masters. They go on holiday abroad, buy houses abroad, school abroad, go for medical treatment abroad, etc. instead of spending this money in their own country to benefit their people.

Statistics show that a Jews' money exchanges hands 18 times before leaving his community while for blacks, it is probably a maximum of once or even zero times.

Only 6% of black money goes back into their community. Therefore, Jews are at the top and blacks are at the bottom of every ladder of society.

Instead of buying Louis Vuitton, Hermes, expensive cars, shoes, houses, dresses and so on, blacks could industrialise Africa, build banks and get rid of colonial institutions by putting them out of business.

> *Interviewer:* What are your thoughts about the failure of blacks after 150 years?
>
> *Jewish leader:* Well, nothing is ever the black man's fault. His compulsive habit of killing his own and material consumption, and his inability to build businesses or preserve wealth is usually somebody else's fault.
>
> *Interviewer:* So, what can blacks do to liberate themselves?
>
> *Jewish leader:* Blacks must take responsibility. Blacks must unite and vehemently fight corrupt leaders who run down their countries and run to IMF as though IMF is Father Christmas.
>
> **Source Unknown**

A Deeper Look

Let us interrogate the above conversation a little deeper, shall we? We will pick on a few statements and expand on them further.

"The only thing blacks understand is consumption."

As per our earlier conversation, we are all as Black people a big fat, ignorant and unsuspecting cash cow for the other races to milk.

- *We do not manufacture or produce anything.*
- *We do not invent much.*
- *We do not wholesale anything.*
- *We do not retail much.*

All we do is come in at the end of the value chain as employees and consumers. It is high time we learned these fundamental truths about wealth:

- *Extracting mineral resources produces wealth.*
- *Manufacturing produces wealth.*
- *Wholesaling produces wealth.*
- *Retailing produces wealth.*
- *Consumption consumes wealth.*

No one has ever become wealthy from consumption.

"The fundamental rule is to keep your money within your racial group. We, the Jews build

Jewish businesses, hire Jewish, buy Jewish and spend Jewish."

This statement should be repeated a thousand times each day until the penny finally drops in our minds. This is a fundamental rule that we need to learn; and in turn, we should engrave this concept in the minds of our children and in those of our grandchildren and all the generations to come. Please!

How long is it going to take for us to appreciate that:

> *The fundamental rule is to keep our money within our racial group. We, Blacks, must build Black businesses, hire Blacks, buy Black and spend Black.*

I look forward to the day when blacks can say the above with confidence and without hesitation.

Keeping our money within our racial group carries the promise that we will build black businesses, employ Black people in their numbers, and spend in a way that broadly empowers black communities.

How long do you think it will take before we master this concept? Five, ten, twenty, fifty or a hundred years? It is difficult to speculate, but if every reader of this book was to start soon after reading it, the future of our children will most assuredly be brighter than our present-day reality.

Remember the ancient Chinese proverb, *"The journey of a thousand miles begins with the first step."* Now let us take the first step my fellow black brothers and sisters.

Remember change starts with us.

"Be the change we want to see"

Mahatma Gandhi

Statistics show that a Jew's money exchanges hands 18 times before leaving his community while for Blacks it is probably a minimum of zero to a maximum of once. Only 6% of black money goes back into their community.

This is us, shooting ourselves in the foot repeatedly and hoping to win the race. It just does not make sense. This generation of Black people has a moral obligation to begin the process of changing the status quo. We must adopt a much more productive and self-empowering manner of participating in the economy.

Circulating only 6% of our income amongst ourselves gives us only a 6% chance of becoming wealthy while we give other races a 94% chance of becoming wealthier, stronger and dominant.

Whichever way you look at it, the odds are significantly stacked against us, yet we continue to make the odds more favourable for every other race by constantly giving them our painfully earned wealth.

The status quo is here to remain until we start spending our money in a way that advances our interests. Nelson Mandela, Malcolm X, Kwame Nkrumah, Dr Martin Luther King Jnr, Robert Mugabe, Samora Machel, Julius Nyerere, Winnie Mandela, Minister Louis Farrakhan and the Honourable Elijah Mohammed have played their part. We must play ours. It is time we stood up and fought for the best economic interests of our communities. Remember the wise words of Steve Bantu Biko, *"Black man you are on your own."*

Let us break it down a bit further. If we only circulate 6% of our income amongst ourselves and spend 94% on other races, it should not be a wonder that our race is in a deplorable and dark economic dungeon. What else could we expect? The writing is on the wall. We are stacking the odds against ourselves and giving other races a 94% chance to succeed for every 6% chance we give ourselves. You are doing this to yourself, Black man. Demons, Satan and the *madlozis* are not responsible for this. It all points back to you! The fault lies squarely on your doorstep! How else do you expect to get ahead economically? With miracle money? Give me a break, *Nigga!* We need to catch a wake-up call. We need to renew our minds and from henceforth think of the dire consequences of our daily decisions!

> *The fundamental rule is to keep our money within our racial group. We, Blacks, must build Black businesses, hire Blacks, buy Black and spend Black.*

The Long-Awaited Redistribution of Wealth

Circulation of money amongst ourselves is the main way to redistribution of wealth in favour of Black people.

- *Toyi-toying has failed us!*
- *Legislation has failed us!*
- *B-BBEE has failed us!*
- *RDP has failed us!*
- *Politicians have failed us!*

Unless we master the concept of circulating money amongst ourselves, we are doomed to economic damnation; consequently, we will remain slaves of the diabolical economic system, and so will the generations to come.

- *Politicians will never address this issue for fear of being politically incorrect.*
- *Politicians are loyal to votes, not equitable redistribution of wealth.*
- *The people who benefit from diabolical economic practices that keep us oppressed are the same people who support our politicians financially.*

- *The wealth distribution responsibility and challenge are for the average person like you and me who are at the grassroots level.*
- *The revolution is squarely on our shoulders.*
- *This can only be a community-driven revolution beginning in the dusty streets of our townships and sweeping across the length and breadth of the continent and the rest of the world.*
- *And this revolution will not be televised!*
- *It will be opposed by white capitalists; however, nothing will stop us!*
- *The countdown towards black economic revolution has begun.*
- *Tick ... Tock ... Tick ... Tock ....*
- *It starts here and now! With you and me!*

Amandla!

4

"IS KAK MAAR IS ORAAIT"

"Black man, run faster or forever remain behind."

Unknown

Is kak maar is oraait" is an old township adage that I grew up hearing. This phrase is used to describe a situation that a person finds repulsive and disgusting but resolves to accept and live with it because they believe they are powerless to change it.

It is a notion so deeply rooted in our subconscious minds as Black people that it encourages an attitude that makes the deplorable acceptable, embracing things that are sickening and abhorrent, and settling for mediocrity and *kak* so to speak.

If change is possible, why settle for *kak*? If good is possible, why settle for better? If best is possible, why settle for good?

Respect for Time

One area in which Black people display disdain for themselves is punctuality. You have surely noticed that Black people have no respect for time whatsoever. Being naturally late for all meetings, events, weddings, funerals and other important activities is a norm.

Other racial groups are surging ahead of us by maximising every second, yet here we are, battling with simple basics like arriving on time for events and meetings. This is a huge disgrace because it indicates that we are failing to manage our time; as a result, our lives. For goodness' sake, we are in the 21st century. We are in the age of technology and speed. If we are to be taken seriously, we must start taking ourselves seriously by learning the value of each second.

> *If change is possible, why settle for kak? If good is possible, why settle for better? If best is possible, why settle for good?*

In Case You Think Everything Is Alright

The White man has been to the moon and has been sending spaceships to Mars and back for years. He has also invented most of the technology we use today. The Chinese have also been making huge strides towards global dominance, so have the Japanese, the Indians and the Arabs; and yet here we are, still struggling with something as elementary as punctuality! *Sies man*!

There is no excuse for such behaviour in the 21st century! What alarms me the most is that we seem to be comfortable with such a repugnant attitude and behaviour regarding time. There is no such thing as African time! This requires a strong rebuke without any apology. ***Wenza ngabomu wena muntu? Mxm!*** You have no excuse for such behaviour!

No Such Thing as African Time!

The fallacy of African time is junk! In the church where I pastor, I have noticed that regardless of how many times I have spoken strongly against late-coming, our people never change their attitudes towards punctuality. Most of our Black people are chronic latecomers who are unwilling to relent and be civilised in their attitude towards time. It is inconceivable how we can be so comfortable with something that degrades and brings us into terrible disrepute, to the point where no one takes us seriously at all because we do not take ourselves seriously.

"We cannot continue to live in a space-age era with a stone-age mentality."

Daryl Davis

Lack of punctuality is a disgrace. Lack of punctuality is backward. Progressive racial groups demonstrate evident respect for time. Punctuality is a virtue they uphold to the highest degree. Those who are always on time are greatly respected and will always be taken seriously in this world. It is also amazing to see how educated Blacks and professionals allow themselves to slide into this intolerable and insulting behaviour.

It appears Black people behave better under the leadership of Whites than they do under black leadership. They are hardly ever late for any activity overseen by a White person but will not respect time under a black overseer.

This shows that something is twisted in our thinking. Time (including how we use it) is the primary determinant of success or failure. If we ever hope to become respectable citizens of this century, we must learn to respect time. In this age, time is money and if we disrespect time, we will never have money.

Most White people respect time, and this is commendable and enviable. Punctuality is a discipline; a lack thereof, shows lack of discipline. Whenever we fail to respect time, we refuse to hold ourselves to a higher standard and a principle of excellence. It is a sign that mediocrity is an acceptable standard to us. Come on Black man, in this competitive 21st century, we cannot subscribe to mediocrity and say, *is kak maar is oraait.*

A Sense of Urgency is Critical

When you consider our unfavourable position, you would think that people who are left behind in the economy and have lost their inheritance, possessions and land would be the ones to run hard and fast to catch up with everyone else. But no, we are passively going about our business as if we are ahead of everyone else.

We are just *"chilled"*, as our kids would say; just taking it easy. We are busy reinforcing stupid adages like, *"There is no hurry in Africa."* Our failure to have a sense of urgency in all that we do is what makes us the laughingstock of the world.

Our passive attitude and relaxed mentality only serve to degrade us. Our tardiness reduces us to characterless people with no vision, urgency or direction. We behave as though the whole world has stopped developing and is waiting for us to catch up. In your dreams, Black man! The world owes you nothing!

As things stand, we are the ones who must run faster or forever remain behind. The rest of the world is ahead of the Black man. We are way behind, and this is no joke. If this does not disturb you, accept that you are simply pathetic.

> *Punctuality is a discipline; a lack thereof, shows lack of discipline. Whenever we fail to respect time, we refuse to hold ourselves to a higher standard and a principle of excellence.*

The Attitude We Should Be Displaying

In the world of sport, the team that is trailing behind tends to be the one that fights harder on all fronts to catch up. They go all out to get back into the game, hoping to win the contest. How we can be so casual on the many serious issues that plague us and still think we can win in the game of life beats me. Why would we be so relaxed while other races are obsessed with improving their efficiency, precision and competitive edge?

We cannot establish order in our societies with a lack of respect for and poor management of time. We are simply laid back and easy-going. Utterly apathetic! We have no sense of urgency in our approach to life.

> *Our tardiness reduces us to characterless people with no vision, urgency or direction. We behave as though the whole world has stopped developing and is waiting for us to catch up.*

Look How Far Behind We Are

I once came across a statement in one of my readings that caused me great concern as I chewed over it. It was recorded like this: *"If Europe was to come to a halt, and stop developing, it would take Africa more than 150 years to catch up with Europe's current level of development and advancement."* Now, as much as I think that this could be another brainwashing attempt into the gospel of *"black is inferior, white is superior"*, I want to plead that for a moment we assume that this statement is true. If it is true, then we should wonder how we could be passive regarding an issue as serious as maximising time.

We must conduct ourselves as if this statement is true. That way, we might change our attitude towards time and punctuality. Maybe that is what we need to develop the urgency to change our ways. *Masingasebenzi ngesikhathi saseAfrika, kufanele sisebenze ngesikhathi sewashi. Ngisho sona leso somlungu!* No such thing as African time!

Self-Introspection

Let us ask ourselves a brutal, and ruthlessly bold question, notwithstanding our history of oppression and slavery which has contributed a lot to our current state of affairs, if our current pace remains, will we ever catch up with the Western world?

For a moment, please stop to consider and ponder upon the general state of our continent, Mother Africa, and compare it to the rest of the world. Where do you honestly think we will be in a decade if we maintained this pace, attitude and trajectory? Will we be at par with our Western and Asian counterparts or further behind? Think about it and ask yourself. Are you justified to continue to behave the way you do about the issues that relate to your progress and development?

I do not know about you, but this brings tears to my eyes. Enough said! Time is a limited resource which we must use wisely, or we will never advance and catch up with the developed world. Once again, heaven please help the Black man!

"You can waste my money, but I will never allow you to waste my time. Money can be recovered but lost time can never be recovered"

Jim Rohn

The Township Tour

To change our ways for the better, we must confront the many unacceptable and abnormal things in our behaviours and communities.

I would like you to imagine with me for a while.

We are driving around on a tour of your township, in the company of a few White, Chinese and Indian people. While driving, we come across a minibus taxi blasting music so loud that it even rattles the windows of other vehicles nearby. If you are anything like me, you are probably wondering how the passengers are coping.

Is this how we treat each other as Black people? Has this madness come to be normal and acceptable? **Hayi bo!**

Then there is another minibus taxi we have been following from the city. All was well while we were on the freeway but as soon as the minibus taxi arrives in the township, we see passengers as well as the driver, opening their windows and throwing out litter.

The same passengers respected the environment when they were in the city, but now that they are in their own township, they feel it is acceptable to throw cans and bottles out the window. As you will agree with me, this is common in your township as well as it is in mine. It is not unusual to see a Black person driving a Cabriolet BMW or Mercedes Benz – both of which are executive cars – throwing out an empty bottle of alcohol from his moving vehicle. It is sheer madness to see a person driving such an expensive, executive and high-quality car behaving like a nonentity. Unfortunately, this is our harsh reality.

God forbid that such a culture of filth and disrespect for our township environment continues to flow down to our offspring. Regardless of whether you are a pedestrian or a driver, whatever car you may be driving, it is unacceptable to litter in your community or anywhere for that matter.

Township Branding

Most of our townships are horribly filthy and repulsively unhygienic. Not because the local authorities are not doing their part but because we do not have any respect for our communities and the environment.

Unfortunately, we have succeeded with flying colours in branding ourselves with filth and litter. **Kak is oraait** around us. It has become our brand. If you were to be driven around Gauteng or any other province in South Africa, one key indicator that you are in a Black township would be the sight of street corners filled with heaps of garbage and litter. You will not travel three blocks without seeing such. What an indictment this is on us as a people. I wonder what other races think of us as they drive around our environment seeing such filth and disgust while we walk around in expensive European labels and drink expensive bottles of whisky. Oh, Black man who has bewitched you?

I do not know about you, but this makes me hang my head in utter shame.

This kind of behaviour cannot be handed down to the next generation – it must stop with us, here and now! Yes, the buck must stop with you!

Do we have such blatant disrespect for our townships? Do we want to keep exposing our children to such disgusting levels of filth that they end up seeing nothing wrong with such *kak*? *God forbid o! I beg o!*

We cannot continue to litter our environment, making it filthy and undesirable to anyone with a sense of self-respect and self-honour. We should take full responsibility and show initiative in ensuring that our township environments are clean, healthy and attractive. It is time we changed. It is time we did some serious self-introspection on this issue. This cannot be delayed.

> *Most of our townships are horribly filthy and repulsively unhygienic. Not because the local authorities are not doing their part but because we do not have any respect for our communities and the environment.*

The State of Our Township Schools

Back to our tour.

We decide to visit a few schools in your township. The first thing we notice is that teachers arrive late for classes while others have the nerve not to pitch up at all.

It is common knowledge that the level of teacher absenteeism and late coming in black schools is unacceptably high. The quality of teaching and learning is significantly far from where it should be. Now hold it right there, let us not play a defensive game because if our township schools were operating at the desired level, we would not have so many thousands of black learners transported in dilapidated buses, mini-buses and *bakkies* in the wee hours of the morning, from our townships to white schools in the nearby suburbs.

We decide to interview a few of the teachers, and while interviewing them we realise that most black teachers live in the same townships that they teach in, but shockingly, their children are being ferried by busses in the early hours of the morning to a white school somewhere.

This picture does not look good at all but that is the reality.

A black teacher staying in a township, teaching in a township school, but enrolling his or her children in a white suburban school is effectively saying to their child: *"I know I am a qualified teacher. I also know well that the quality of my teaching is poor and so I cannot allow you to be taught by my colleagues or myself. But do not worry; I know a white school in a suburb 50 kilometres away from our township where they deliver better quality tuition than my colleagues and I can give. I would rather entrust you into the white teacher's care than my own. They will do a much better job in educating you than I can because* **they are superior and I am inferior***. Even though you* *may lose your soul and Africanness in this whole process, it is a risk I am willing to take."*

This is a sad situation. I am speechless. *Selah.*

On the other hand, the black township teacher is saying to the white teacher: *"I concede that you are superior and I am inferior. You can do a far better job educating my children than I can. My children are better off in your care than they are in mine. Continue to teach my children while I will give poor quality tuition to black learners whose parents have no option but to send their children to the non-fee-paying school I teach in because of their socio-economic plight."*

Such is the attitude and mindset of our black educators working in our township schools.

The State of Our Health Care Services

From there, off we move on to the hospitals in your township. What immediately strikes us are the unfriendly and rude attitudes displayed by black healthcare staff towards black patients, including elderly patients.

Now that is **kak** to the power of ten!

> *Masingasebenzi ngesikhathi saseAfrika, kufanele sisebenze ngesikhathi sewashi. Ngisho sona leso somlungu!*

I have friends and relatives who have been admitted to both public hospitals in townships as well as public hospitals in predominantly white areas. They indicated to me that the quality of service rendered to black patients in white public hospitals is significantly better than the quality of service rendered to black patients in public hospitals within black communities. You may have probably noticed or experienced the same.

If there is any truth to these allegations, then the question that we need to answer as Black people is, when, how and why did we deteriorate to such a deplorable state of apathy and scorn that we cannot even treat our sick with respect and dignity? We seem to forget that the sick people we mistreat are the same taxpayers paying our salaries on an ongoing basis.

#IsKakMaarIsOraaitMustFall!

It comes as no surprise that many Black people would rather pay for the expensive services of a White man than support a fellow Black man. This is because of the bad experiences with black service providers. They received poor service, and in some instances, the service providers ran off with the paid money without completing the project. Many of us can tell a story or two about this. I have burnt my fingers several times too.

Again, the question is, when, how and why did we deteriorate to this appalling state of apathy? Why are we being forced by our own fellow black service providers' incompetence and lack of professionalism to trust our former oppressors and colonisers? How do we even circulate money amongst ourselves when we offer such deplorable service to one another?

The urgency of the hour demands that we do whatever it takes to restore our pride and dignity as a people by ending black mediocrity. We need to understand that whatever we do is not just an individual action to get through the day, but a representation of the state of the black mind.

When you and I deliver on our promise and exceed our customer's or clients' expectations, we raise the flag of our race. It also presents to us an excellent opportunity to dispel the many stereotypes held about Black people – that Black people are incapable of service excellence and can only deliver *kak*. It is time that we changed and restored our self-respect and dignity as Black people. We must do away with this *"Is kak maar is oraait"* mentality. We need to remember that respect and honour are earned; they do not just fall from a tree.

"Excellence honours God and inspires people."

Bill Hybels

Enough is Enough

The absence of excellence in the way we operate, handle our environment, and render services to one another is an indictment on us and one of the main causes of many of our problems. We will never sell our services to other races with such a deplorable attitude towards service excellence.

Shooting Ourselves in the Foot

Some time ago, I visited a government department to get some assistance. It was just after lunchtime when I met a Black brother who was supposed to serve me. He arrogantly told me that he is full and never works when he has just had lunch. I thought he was joking, so I waited a little bit longer for him but to no avail. He proved that he was not joking. I did not get help from him that day.

Since this was an important issue, I made my way back there the next day and I arrived before lunch. Lo and behold, I found the same guy and he attended to me speedily. I could not believe that the same person who could not assist me the day before was done helping me within minutes. With this kind of lousy attitude towards work and service, you can be certain that we are headed nowhere very fast. Before we can even think about building our economy and circulating money amongst ourselves, we need to confront issues poor service and address them with the strongest possible measures. We have a moral obligation to restore the dignity of our race and leave this world a better place than we found it, for the sake of our children.

> *We need to understand that whatever we do is not just an individual action to get through the day, but a representation of the state of the black mind.*

Who Can Respect Such Kak?

Respect and honour are not basic human rights which everyone is entitled to. If we are to be treated with respect by politicians, service providers, educators, and health care workers, we should demand that we are served with the excellence we deserve. A substandard and mediocre attitude is not going to cut it. Mediocrity must never be an acceptable standard to live by. We have shown and proven over many decades that we are comfortable with mediocrity; hence the world is treating us with disdain and contempt.

Mediocrity has become our portion because we do not value ourselves. The problem with the Black person is that he has always believed that he deserves *kak*. We hardly ever complain when we receive bad service from each other. We accept substandard products and poor-quality service even when we have paid dearly for them because to us *kak* is acceptable.

We never do anything about the nauseating litter and filth in our townships. We never challenge each other and hold ourselves accountable to higher standards of excellence. We never push each other to improve our communities and be innovative in our businesses. Instead, we applaud and promote mediocrity.

The reason we do not do anything to improve our communal flaws is that somewhere in our subconscious minds we have a weird belief that the best is not meant for us. We approach life with apathy because we have accepted substandard as norm; hence we believe that *is kak maar is oraait*. Not anymore. *Is kak en is nie oraait nie!* Black mediocrity must fall – the sooner it does, the better for our race! It begins with you.

Remember, we are fearfully and wonderfully made in the image of our Creator. Let us not tarnish His image.

> *We have shown and proven over many decades that we are comfortable with mediocrity; hence the world is treating us with disdain and contempt.*

The Race of Races

I would like us to take some time and look at the dictionary meaning of the word *"race."* There are two dictionary meanings of this word which I would like us to look at.

The first is *"a contest of speed, as in running, riding, driving or sailing."*

The second is *"a group of persons related by common descent or heredity."*

In the context of how the world works, we can combine the two definitions and deduct that a race is *a contest or competition, between groups of persons related by common descent or heredity.*

Bringing it closer home, it would mean that the different races – Black, White, Indian and Asian

– are in a race, competing hard to get ahead and achieve supremacy.

The race is real and none of the races wants to be left behind except for the Black race. It is as though we gladly volunteer to be left behind while pushing others ahead of us.

This means that Whites are running faster to stay ahead in economic and political power, education, technology contests and others. The Asians, Indians and other races are treading closer to the heels of the Whites. The question which is, are Black people taking this race seriously?

There is no doubt that Whites, Chinese, Japanese and Indians are running as if their lives depended on it. Some races like the Japanese, Chinese and Koreans have even managed to come from behind and caught up with the Europeans and eventually overtook them.

One day that could be our story too.

When Races Are Serious

A hundred years ago, no one thought China and Japan would be strong contenders in the global economy. Nevertheless, they are now.

Rated the second and third-largest economies in the world respectively, they have managed to outrun all European countries including Germany and the United Kingdom. This is what happens when a race pulls together and takes themselves, their languages, cultures, economies and the race of races seriously!

Today, Toyota, a Japanese motor company, is the largest producer and seller of vehicles in the world. They learned the skills from America and are now giving the USA a run for pole position as a global superpower. This shows that you can come from behind, catch up and lead if you are serious about your race and its position in this race of races.

My fellow Black brother let us be brutally honest with each other and ask ourselves this question, are we taking this race seriously enough to be considered serious contenders in the global space? Or are we expecting this stew to be cooked and served to us on a silver platter?

No race can assert itself in the global village if it does not take itself seriously enough to cook its own stews.

The Japanese went to America, learned to cook the American stew and went back home to improve on it. Now they prepare better stews than America. That is what we should do as the Black nation. But alas, we are still battling with rudimentary issues like embracing our own culture, language and heritage. We are yet to master basics like punctuality, rendering excellent service, circulating money amongst ourselves and respecting and supporting one another.

Morena re hauhele. Lord have mercy on us.

We are not ready to be respected as a people because we do not respect ourselves. We need to have a meeting amongst ourselves, look each other in the eye, and have brutal, honest, confrontational, ruthless, and gloveless conversations with one another. We must correct this nonsense, lest our ignoble disposition continues until kingdom come.

The Black man you see in the mirror is the one I am challenging you to confront first. When you see the state of a Black man's situation, whether good or bad, you are seeing a mirror reflection of yourself. You can either resolve to ignore what you see and walk away, or you can begin to improve what that mirror reflects.

> *We never push each other to improve our communities and be innovative in our businesses. Instead, we applaud and promote mediocrity.*

Passing on the Baton

We need to consider ourselves as running a relay race against other races. It is not just about the current generation but also about our children who will either be advantaged or disadvantaged by our performance in this race. By the time we hand over the baton to them, we would have set them up to either win or lose the race. It all depends on how fast we run our leg or stage of the race. Whether the other races stay ahead of us or not is directly related to our determination and performance as we run.

If we perform poorly, we will not be the only ones who suffer the repercussions of being left behind – our children and the generations that follow will suffer the most and that is not what we want.

My heart races like a wild horse each time I think and reflect on these issues.

Our Race Against the World

Compared to other races that are already far ahead, we are a joke. They are far ahead of us, yet they run as if they are the ones trailing behind. This they do so that they can put their children further ahead, giving them a huge advantage over the children of our race.

White people, Jews, Asians and others have already positioned their children to run the world economy and acquire an even bigger share of the world's wealth.

This means Black people must run like mad people on steroids. If we do not, we are at risk of becoming enslaved again. Even though the methods of slavery would be different this time, the results would be the same. May God grant us the wisdom to *"wake up and smell the coffee.'* It is about time we did.

Are you beginning to sweat as we discuss these pertinent matters? I must admit that I am. Excuse me while I grab a towel, I need to wipe my sweaty palms and dry my teary eyes.

> *Compared to other races that are already far ahead, we are a joke. They are far ahead of us, yet they run as if they are the ones trailing behind.*

Our Untapped Advantage

As for us, the Black people of South Africa, we already have an advantage that we may not be aware of – we are the backbone of the economy. As stated in the previous chapters, the economy of South Africa rests on the buying power of Black people. So, we just need to be smart and do what we need to do to surge ahead. **Tadaah!**

We must be willing to work as slaves and spend our money within our communities and teach our children to do the same so that our offspring and their generations can live like kings. ***Selah!***

So, come on now Black man, put on your work suit and do away with your self-defeating habits. Start supporting your brother and stop apportioning blame to Whites. For as long as you continue to apportion blame to someone else, you give up the power to change. Black man, you have no choice but to run faster or be forever left behind! Come on, let us do it!

Why We Must Win this Race

This race is crucial because whoever reaches the finish line first will be the leader, master, employer and controller of all those that come in behind.

As for the ones who come last, they will be relegated to slaves of every other race.

As harsh as it sounds, it is unfortunately how this world operates and has been operating like this since time immemorial.

The rules of the world will never change to suit our black complacency.

Black man, you have no choice but to run faster or forever remain a modern-day slave.

Selah! Selah! Selah!

Back to Sankomota, I pray that the lyrics of this timeless song shake us out of the nonchalance we have been displaying. It is now or never.

Now or Never

Sankomota

Heyi wena Afrika

Kgale o dutse hae

Tsamaya o lo ipatlela sa bophelo

Tsoha o iketsetse

Heyi wena Afrika

Kgale o dutse hae

Tsamaya o lo ipatlela tsa bophelo

Tsoha o iketsetse

Vuka baba vuka

Life has been passing you by

Follow your star it's now or never

Hayi you've got to make it better

Heyi wena Afrika

Kgale u dutse hae

Tsamaya o lo ipatlela tsa bophelo

Tsoha o iketsetse

Vuka baba, vuka

Life has been passing you by

Follow your star it's now or never

Hayi you've got to make it better

O dutse o phuthile matsoho (dutse o phuthile)

Afrika, hae lale (hae lale)

O re o shebile ntho tsa mahala

You gonna wait forever

O dutse o phuthile matsoho (dutse o phuthile)

Afrika, hae lale (Hae lale)

O re o shebile ntho tsa mahala

You gonna wait forever

O phutile matsoho

O shebile banna ha ba sebetsa

Wena

O phutile matsoho

O shebile banna ha ba sebetsa

Wena

O phutile matsoho

O shebile banna ha ba sebetsa

Wena

O phutile matsoho

O shebile banna ha ba sebetsa

Wena

O phutile matsoho

O shebile banna ha ba sebetsa

Wena

O phutile matsoho

O shebile banna ha ba sebetsa

Wena

I rest my case.

Please play this song on repeat, all day for seven days until the penny drops.

I am watching you.

5

DO BLACKS LOVE THEMSELVES?

"Black man you are on your own"

Steve Bantu Biko

Kenneth and Mamie Clark, a black American couple, who were both psychologists, published three major papers between 1939 and 1940 on children's self-perception as it related to race. Their studies found that African American children attending black-only schools would choose a white doll over a black doll when given a choice between the two. To explain their choice, the children stated that the white doll was nicer, and the black doll was ugly. This study concluded that the response of the sampled children reflected the acute self-hatred amongst black children, thus their tendency to prefer white to black.

Is it not shocking how black parents can swiftly transfer their sense of inferiority and self-hate onto their children? It is mind-boggling that a black child, whose mind is supposed to be innocent and neutral, will at an early age portray an endemic sense of black inferiority and aspire towards whiteness.

Surely, it must have been transferred from parents through socialisation. It makes me wonder whether this scenario is still playing itself out to this day, only that now it is prevalent and chronic amongst the adult black populace.

The Fallacy of Black Inferiority

"What you know, I also know; I am not inferior to you."

Job 13 v 2

If a Black man had a choice to be served by either a White man or a Black man, they will most likely choose the White man over the Black man. I am saying this because there are many instances that indicate that Black people still think that being white is better than being black. Some Black people still believe that things done by Whites are superior or better in quality while Blacks (in their eyes) can only produce inferior goods or services.

This gives the White man an added, unfair and effortless advantage over the Black man, in all spheres of life probably.

Over and over, without even assessing the long-term impact of their choices, the Black man's default preference is the White man's service, even when opting for the Black man would offer superior results.

The evidence of my assertion above is all around us. If you don't believe me, let's look at the common choices below made by Black adults.

- *We prefer white schools to black schools.*
- *We prefer the White man's English language to our mother tongues.*

- *We prefer white businesses to black businesses. And yes, I had to say it again.*
- *We prefer white fashion to our native styles.*
- *We prefer white churches to black churches.*
- *We prefer white-led political parties to black-led political parties.*
- *We prefer white residential areas to black-dominated areas.*
- *We prefer straight hair to the tight kinky curls of black hair. I can't believe some even have the guts to buy straight hair and wear it.*
- *We prefer white culture to black culture.*
- *We prefer white accents to South African mother tongue decorated accents.*
- *We prefer white mannerisms to African mannerisms.*
- *We prefer white cuisine to our culinary traditions.*

The list goes on and on.

Black Migration

I am a Black man who still stays in a township by choice. Out of choice, black pride and preference, I remain in a black township. Now, please do not misconstrue my words, there is nothing wrong with staying in or moving to a suburb. ***However, I*** *think there is everything wrong in thinking that migrating to a white community will elevate your status and sense of importance.*

Moving to the burbs should be motivated by affordability and the convenience of being closer to your place of work or business operations – not by a sense of *"good riddance"* to that place infested with Black people who remind you of a past you are working so hard to run from.

After all, South Africa belongs to all who live in it, anyone can choose to live anywhere they please. However, this should never be done to distance yourself from blackness. I could move to a suburb, if I wanted to, without having a sense of escaping my blackness and pursuing neo-whiteness.

South Africa is my country, and I can choose to stay wherever I want without despising my roots and betraying my identity.

My loyalty and sense of indebtedness are to plough back into my township through activities that uplift our Black people, especially our youth.

Disconnecting from your roots as a means of upgrading your status is foolishness because you will always be identified by who you are and never by where you stay.

You can be the only Black man in an all-white neighbourhood but that does not upgrade you to a new identity or give you an honorary white status.

Black migration into white suburbs is not a sign of progress and advancement. When we view it through such a lens, we are simply affirming a self-imposed sense of inferiority.

By migrating to the burbs, we are simply hijacking the progress made by White people in building their communities. There is no progress for us there. Even if we all moved to the suburbs and the population there became 100% black, we cannot claim that as advancement.

It is only when we cook our own stews by developing our townships into more enviable communities that we can say we are making progress. Therefore, when we do well financially as Black people, we must cultivate a sense of responsibility towards our communities before we flee to white suburbs. We should refuse to selfishly rise to economic strength as individuals. We should instead be about collective progress.

Purpose as a Black man, to pull others along just as the Jews, Chinese and Indians do. They do not take pride in individual success; they pursue collective success with everything within them. A lesson Black people still need to learn. So, help us, God!

You can choose to live wherever you want. But check your motives when you make this decision. Lest you sell your souls for a bowl of soup.

> *Disconnecting from your roots as a means of upgrading your status is foolishness because you will always be identified by who you are and never by where you stay.*

Black Self-Hate

"Who taught you to hate the colour of your skin? Who taught you to hate the texture of your hair? Who taught you to hate the shape of your nose

and the shape of your lips? Who taught you to hate yourself from the top of your head to the soles of your feet? Who taught to hate your own kind? Who taught you to hate the race that you belong to so much that you don't want to be around each other?"

Malcolm X

Around the time I conceived the idea of this book in 2015, South Africa was in the worst-ever throes of xenophobic violence. Black people were burning and killing one other in the nastiest and most barbaric manner imaginable. Scenes from the violence told a story of degeneration from mere dislike of each other to detestation. Sadly, this was not the first display of our despise and disrespect for one another. These distasteful feeling towards each have led to a polarised Black nation.

Have you noticed that even in our business endeavours we do not support each other? A Black man will throughout his lifetime embark on endeavours that fail because of lack of support and encouragement from his fellow Black people. On the contrary, we are famous for pulling each other down and sabotaging one another's efforts. Instead of accepting that *"Your success is my honour"*, we hold tightly to, *"Your success is my offence thus witchcraft"*.

We seem committed to ensuring that anything and everything black must fail. We are a shameless lot who keep shooting ourselves in the foot, forgetting that our negative attitude and behaviour towards each other is tantamount to self-assassination.

However, when a Black man dies, thousands travel from near and far, bravely cross the wildest rivers, just to see him sink six feet under the soil. The same people who could not buy a fifty-rand product in support of a black brother's hustle will move mountains to attend his funeral. We seem to care for our fellow Blacks when they are dead than when they are alive.

- *Where does such a repugnant degree of self-hatred come from?*
- *Why do we have a loathful attitude towards our race?*
- *Why do we despise our race so much that at every opportunity we desire to escape blackness as if it is a curse?*

- *Have we become so uncomfortable in the castles of our skin that we believe we need a White man's affirmation for us to appreciate ourselves?*

> **We should refuse to selfishly rise to economic strength as individuals.**

Black Self-Love

My intention in this chapter is to promote black self-love, black self-acceptance, black self-prioritisation and black self-preference.

I am aware that the views I share in this book could be misinterpreted as racist ideologies, but I want to categorically state, that this is not about racism. It is all about Black people loving themselves enough to put their interests above those of other races. This is about black self-love. It is about restoring to the Black man a love for self that is so strong that he will prefer his blackness above anything that represents whiteness and all that has to do with it. It is about affirming that as a people we are not in any way inferior to any other race.

Until we learn to love and embrace ourselves as authentic human beings, created in the image and likeness of God, we will struggle to work together and achieve the tangible progress we need. We cannot continue to hate one another, Black man! No, we cannot! We must love ourselves and love each other.

Our preference for other races is rooted in our self-hate. Listen *muntu omnyama,* you and I are not inferior to the Whites, the Arabs, the Indians or the Chinese in any way. We are not! Say it with me: *I am not inferior to a white person or any other race for that matter!*

Disrespect for Black Authority

When a White person becomes a leader over Black people, their black subordinates afford them due respect. On the other hand, when a Black person becomes a leader over his fellow Black people, discontentment, bickering, gossip and even curses are used as weapons to bring the black leader down. The root cause of this anomaly is our deep-seated sense of self-hatred.

I remember my first job after serving my articles with an accounting firm. I was a supervisor within the finance department where I had both black and white subordinates reporting directly to me. From time to time, I would request that my juniors run photocopies for me. Whenever I requested Whites to do so (some of whom were much older than I was), it was hardly a problem.

Then one day, I requested a fellow black brother, much younger than I was and the lowest in rank within the department to make copies for me. His response was: *"Eeh, utlwa monyimbi o a reng"* – meaning, this is crazy, I can't believe that this *Nigga* is asking me to make photocopies for him! The question now becomes, if Black people could openly disrespect each other to such a degree, then who must honour them? White people? I leave this to your capable brain.

Do Whites Like Blacks?

I am exposed to the Charismatic/Pentecostal way of doing church as I am part of it. I have noticed a strong trend in that movement, Black people tend to move from black churches to join white-led churches in droves.

This trend has grown so exponentially that you even find Black people who live in townships travelling long distances on Sundays to worship in white suburban churches.

Many Black people who have relocated to white suburbs will naturally, conveniently, and gladly join white churches. Many of those white churches have moved from 95% white membership to 95% black membership in a very short space of time.

To verify this for yourself, take some time to watch South African church programmes on television stations like TBN, Faith Network and Daystar, which feature various prominent, white-led churches. Pay careful attention to the white-led churches from South Africa and within minutes, you will see what I am talking about. A white pastor and his white leadership team lead a church whose membership is over 90% black and even higher in some cases.

Let us Interrogate This Further

What has been happening is what we can call *"white flight"* – where the more Black people join white churches, the more White people leave those churches. As stated before, the membership composition of some of those churches has moved from 95% white to 95% black.

The question we keep avoiding is, why would a composition of a church take such a dramatic turn? Did White people die or disappear suddenly when Black people joined those churches? *Was there a rapture that only targeted White people and excluded Black people?* Or did they feel so overwhelmed and overcrowded by the invasion of Black people that they eventually resorted to leaving their multi-million-rand air-conditioned facilities, which they built with their hard-earned money?

Is their intolerance for Black people so strong that it would cause them to leave their legacy in fear of being suffocated by Black people?

Could this, by any chance, be the reflection of the magnanimous dislike Whites have for Black people? I will leave it to you to answer all these questions.

Please think about these questions as honestly as possible. There is no need for you to fast and pray for a revelation from God because it is plain to see. Just apply your mind and think long, deep, and hard.

> *Why do we despise our race so much that at every opportunity, we desire to escape blackness as if it were a curse?*

Kumbaya

Wait a minute. Aren't Christians, both black and white, supposed to live in perfect harmony singing *"kumbaya my Lord, kumbaya"* around a bon fire until Christ returns?

You could be asking, *"Is there anything wrong when Black people join white churches?"* You are asking the wrong question my friend. The question you should be asking is, *"Why are Whites leaving their churches in throngs as soon as Black people join them?"*

The disturbing issue is that only Black people leave their black churches to join white churches.

It never happens that White people leave their white churches to join black churches. There are many great churches led by competent and honourable black pastors that are within the walking distances of both the black and white residences; but both races will choose a church led by a white pastor.

The *"rule of thumb"* these days is, a white pastor involuntarily attracts a lot of black worshippers whose continual flow into the church eventually drives away white worshippers – which I assume must be very frustrating to the white pastor. **Askies Pastoor!**

On the other side, even the most gifted black pastor will hardly ever attract any white members. Are the results of the white versus black dolls study from Kenneth and Mamie Clark's research papers also playing out in our churches? Do Black people, consciously or unconsciously prefer white churches over black churches?

You be the judge!

I find it inconceivable that a Black person would prefer his former oppressor to a fellow Black brother. This to me is a mystery that only eternity might one day reveal to me.

Mutation

Some white churches have gone to the extent of having a separate Afrikaans and English service. The Afrikaans speaking congregants attend their service and the English congregation has its own. Could it be that the Afrikaans service is predominantly attended by the preferred membership as opposed to the English service, which is attended mainly by the invaders? Please do not frown and roll your eyes, I am only asking a sincere question. Anyway, you must still do your math and solve x.

Shall we rock this boat a bit more? In the unlikely event that a highly gifted young black pastor is appointed as a successor to a white senior pastor of one of these white churches, do you think that the few remaining white members would stay plugged into that church and serve faithfully under the leadership of the black pastor? You be the judge of that too.

Eish, my apologies for making you feel uncomfortable. It is just the plain truth, and it must be told so that you may be set free.

My observation is that Whites do not serve comfortably under black leadership. They detest serving under a black leader because they feel superior to Black people, yet through our actions, we are always ready to affirm the two-sided lie of white superiority and black inferiority. This is a tendency that applies not only in churches but also in other aspects of our interactions.

> *I find it inconceivable that a Black person would prefer his former oppressor to a fellow Black brother. This to me is a mystery that only eternity might one day reveal to me.*

When Blacks Land, Whites Take Off

There are two things I would like us to talk about. One, is the feeling Black people have when they are in the company of Whites. The other, is the feeling White people have when they are in the company of Black people.

Black people generally feel a sense of affirmation, prestige and honour when they are in the company of White people. They feel as though they have arrived and have finally made it. They feel as though they have earned bragging rights over fellow backward Black brothers and sisters who are not part of the exclusive community that they are now a part of.

On the other hand, White people feel uncomfortable when Black people are in their space. They feel invaded, smothered and overcrowded. They feel a general sense of decline in their value, quality and prestige. If there are a few Black people around them, they feel that they have given these privileged Blacks a rare opportunity to be amongst them. Black people see this as honour; white people view it as devaluation.

Before you scream foul, let us look at a few examples that will elucidate my submissions.

Blacks in White Suburbs

About 25 kilometres away from my township Soshanguve, is a suburb called The Orchards, which was approximately 95% white twenty or so years ago. As Black people started moving into the suburb, White people fled the area. Fast forward two decades later, The Orchards is now sitting at approximately 97% black occupancy. Did the Whites die? Did Black people just move in to occupy their empty houses? No, the more Black people came in, the more Whites sold their houses as they fled black invasion.

Bitter tablet?

Swallow it because that is the liberating truth!

Blacks in White Schools

An interesting trend I have seen keeps playing out in white suburban schools. When the school's black learner population begins to increase, white parents are quick to transfer their kids from these schools as they flee black infiltration. To them, the infiltration of Black people spells chaos and disorder.

The fact remains, our love for proximity to whiteness is a mystery I find difficult to fathom.

Is this pseudo-progress worth selling the souls of our children so they grow up with a white-is-better mentality? Nonsense! *Twak!*

Not too far from where I live is a school called Haakdoorn Primary School. At some point, it had a 100% white teaching staff and a 100% white learner base. Today 100% of its learners are black, but the teachers remain predominantly white. The more Black children came in, the more the white parents removed their children. Another school that comes to mind is Loreto Convent School in Pretoria. Two decades ago, most of its learners were white; now the school is almost 100% black with white teachers constituting most of the staff. The question remains, do Whites want Black people in their space?

Black Honour Must Rise

Our sense of worth and value should never be derived from how White people feel about us. Being disliked by Whites should not be an issue for Black people. Just as the Chinese do not seek white affirmation, neither should Black people. Just as the Arabs do not seek white acceptance, neither should Black people. Just as the Japanese do not seek white approval, neither should Black people. Blacks are the only group of people who clamour after white acceptance and affirmation. This happens so much it has become an addiction that we have passed on to our children. Instead of seeking white acceptance, we must be cultivating a sense of black pride and honour, especially amongst our children.

White people do not like us, but that is not the issue and it should never be. We should not even care what they think or feel about us. The real issue should be our self-love and self-acceptance. If we fail to love ourselves, how can we expect other races to display an inch of capacity to love and accept us? It is far-fetched and beyond far-fetched. It is impossible. We must stop looking to graduate from being black to achieving an honorary white status. *Sefoet man!*

The crux of the matter is, let us love, accept and promote each other. This should come more naturally than seeking white approval.

History Attests to the Fact

Exhibit 1: University of the Free State

In 2008, the University of the Free State in Bloemfontein, hogged the headlines because of a racism scandal that took place on its campus. A group of racist white kids opposed the so-called racial integration in the student residences. To manifest their defiance, they recorded a video that went viral on social media, which showed them lining up gullible black workers from the university and forcing them to crawl on their knees, eat out of buckets and drink urine, and shout self-degrading recitations which exalted White people. As we all know, the scandal dragged on and on without resolution, until the appointment of Professor Jonathan Jansen as the University's Vice-Chancellor. Professor Jansen later met with Julius Malema and the rest was history.

Exhibit 2: *University of Cape Town*

The year 2015 saw the *"#RhodesMustFall"* campaign. It was sparked by black students at the University of Cape Town to alert the nation about the high levels of racial intolerance demonstrated by White people at that university. Twenty-one years after freedom, the university had not transformed at all. It still operated like the traditional whites-only colonialist institution it had always been. The black students demanded the removal of the statue of Cecil John Rhodes that occupied a prominent position at the campus. The statue was eventually removed but did white supremacist attitudes fall? I have my doubts.

Exhibit 3: Curro – Roodeplaat

When Panyaza Lesufi was appointed as Member of the Executive Committee (MEC) of Education for the Gauteng Province in South Africa, his first major crisis was to deal with the racist attitudes displayed by white teachers towards black pupils at Curro School in Roodeplaat, Pretoria.

It emerged that kids were being separated in their classrooms along racial lines. The school apologised and everyone moved on, but before the dust could settle, a video was leaked from the same school. Teachers were caught on camera, separating children based on their race on a bus during a school trip.

The MEC had to crack the whip on the management again. He threatened to cancel the school's operating licence. Again, the school profusely apologised, but was there any change of heart in their attitude towards black pupils? Maybe we should ask Jan Van Riebeck and Hendrick Verwoerd, they might be able to shed some light.

> *Blacks are the only group of people who clamour after white acceptance and affirmation.*

Now that We Know

These are only a few of the sporadic cases that saw daylight in the media. Heinous acts of this nature perpetrated by White people against Black people are taking place quietly in many other different institutions and environments across our country. This is the loudest statement from most White people in South Africa: *"We don't want Black people in our space!"*

I am sure we can all agree that actions speak louder than words; and so far, White people's actions have been unequivocal in their message towards us. They are screaming with the loudest and clearest public address systems available, their actions.

The actions of certain pockets of white supremacist movements expose their attitudes regarding Black people – their deepest and truest feelings about the Black man.

They do not like a Black man, and they do not want a Black man in their space. We are a threat to their comfort. The more of us they see around them, the more uncomfortable they feel. They feel as though walls are closing in on them. They feel suffocated by a Black man.

Askies tog asseblief for *making you White fellows feel that way. The Black man is not going anywhere. This is his country.*

And to you my fellow Black man, I just shared a few examples of how Whites prefer their own space and how they feel *"oppressed"* by the constitution of our country. The dream of a rainbow nation is asking too much of them; to foster peace by integrating with Black people is too much an ask. So far some have tolerated the dream.

The question I have for Black people is, which is better, to be tolerated by Whites or to be appreciated by your own? I certainly would not like to be in an environment where I am merely tolerated. I am fearfully and wonderfully made in the image of God. I will never settle for being tolerated. I am to be celebrated and appreciated! Full stop! Finish and *klaar*! I am Black and I am proud of it. No White person will change the way I feel about myself.

Quality Questions Yield Quality Answers

One of the reasons we are still clueless is because we ask all the wrong questions. As you would know, the quality of questions we ask determines the quality of answers we can ever hope to get. Up to now, the only question we have asked ourselves is, why are White people refusing to change? We have not asked: what must we, as Black people, do about our situation?

The latter is the question we should tackle as Black people. Running after White people and forcing ourselves down their throats will not help us.

The answer to the latter question is simple: we need to love and value ourselves, come together behind a common agenda, and start building ourselves; and thereafter, our institutions of excellence. We need to also improve the environment we live in and restore dignity to our communities so they can be enviable.

The power to do this lies more in our hands than in the hands of the Government. If we move in one direction and make a bold statement, the Government will have no choice but to come to the table and play its part.

We Are the Change

Not all change must be pioneered by Government. Change begins at the grassroots and comes through the collective and coordinated actions of the masses. We can start with gatherings of great minds amongst us, from the community level up to national level. From these engagements, we can chart and commit to a plan of action. These gatherings will ultimately culminate into a broader citizens' movement.

Let us look and learn from the organisations that seek to preserve white Afrikaners such as *Afriforum, Afrikaner Broederbond* and *Solidaridiet*. These are not political parties but movements that seek to give direction, cast vision, and go to war for the Afrikaner agenda. The day we start such, is the day we would have won half the battle. The rest will be a matter of alignment and action. Truth be told, I envy these Afrikaner movements. Isn't it time Black people had similar organisations?

The Afrikaners did this when they established their *Afrikaner Broederbond*. It is time we established our *Ubuntubond*.

B4 Loading...

Time for Black Excellence

The raw truth has been established —Whites do not like Black people – it is important to stop running after them and their establishments. Let's start building our great businesses, schools, churches and estates.

Now that we realise that ready-made stew is not as delicious as it appears to be, let us liberate ourselves mentally by acting decisively on these burning issues.

In Mzansi, we have a common practice of following White people wanting to be part of their social structures. This is understandable because there are many things that we need that were only accessible and open to White people and not to us, thus justifying our desire to go after them.

We are human; as such, we have the right to aspire greater and better things just like every other people group. It is only natural for us to desire the finer things. We do not have these things in our communities because of the imbalances created by apartheid. White people – who were privileged and benefited under apartheid – have all these things at their disposal. This truth explains much of the migration of our people from black to white communities.

Nevertheless, what we have seen over the years is that Black people are met with rejection and contempt in white spaces. They are looked down upon as substandard humans who should only be tolerated and never embraced. Whites become uncomfortable when they have to share space with Black people. The management of these institutions will also quietly acknowledge that they have a problem on their hands. In this mixed confusion, Black people begin to receive undignified treatment. They are insulted and referred to by the "k" word – whether audibly or silently, it is the cold truth. Black people are subtly segregated from key positions, events and activities.

I believe Whites do not want us invading their spaces, neighbourhoods, institutions and fraternities. My question to you is, are you going to waste your time trying so hard to fit in with such people? Should we be wasting time *toyi-toying* in pursuit of affirmation and approval from such cowards who do not want to see the playing field levelled because they fear losing their unjustified privilege?

> ***Which is better, to be tolerated by Whites or to be appreciated by your own?***

Talk is Cheap, Black Man

We must stop talking about transformation and integration and shift the conversation to the possession of maximum control of our destiny and fate.

We need to start producing the goods we consume; the bread and mealie meal we eat; the clothes we wear; and the drinks we enjoy. We need to chart a plan to build the institutions we need. Then and only then, will we ever enter our Promised Land and Black Paradise, which flows with milk and honey.

6

BLACK MAN SET YOUR MIND FREE!

"Emancipate yourselves from mental slavery, none but ourselves can free our minds."

Robert Nester Marley

Artist Unknown

As the saying goes, *"A picture is worth a thousand words"*.

The story told by the picture below cuts deep. This picture depicts what we need to do to liberate ourselves after all the psychological damage caused by slavery, colonisation, oppression, marginalisation and apartheid.

These systems made us believe that we are inferior, backward and incapable of significant achievements. They further indoctrinated us and made us believe that our purpose in this world is to serve White people and other nations as dependent slaves. They also taught us that our survival, advancement and development are at the mercy of other races.

This picture communicates a profound message. It makes it clear that the Black man must liberate himself by breaking the chains of slavery, colonisation and apartheid *in his mind*. Overcoming the enslaving myth that Black people are inferior to other races can only happen when the Black man sets his psyche free from this lie.

As long as we do not consciously challenge these blatant lies, we will forever think, feel and believe what the people who seek to continually oppress us desire. **Only the Black man's mind and willpower can set him free from these bonds.**

The delusion that Blacks must always suck up to other races for affirmation can only be broken when we exercise the power of our minds. The enslaving spending patterns of Black people can only be broken when Black people liberate themselves from mental slavery.

"Emancipate Yourselves from Mental Slavery"

We can never be free until we succeed in liberating ourselves mentally. Constitutional liberation was necessary but incomplete in and of itself. It is dangerous to be liberated on paper but still be enslaved mentally. Constitutional liberation without mental liberation will still yield the oppressor's desired results, particularly economic marginalisation.

> *The delusion that Blacks must always suck up to other races for affirmation can only be broken when we exercise the power of our minds.*

Dispelling the Myth

The myth that Black people are the weak majority and Whites are the strong minority must be dispelled. Where have you ever seen the majority weak and the minority strong? Only a mentally weak and helpless majority can allow this abnormal status quo to exist. You will never see this in America, China or Japan. The majority is never weak.

It is only in Africa where the majority serves the minority because we have been enslaved in our minds. But our generation has begun undoing this crazy and disempowering myth.

> *Constitutional liberation without mental liberation will still yield the oppressor's desired results, particularly economic marginalisation.*

Liberate Your Mind

A story is told of an elephant whose leg had been chained for some time. The chain restricted the elephant's movements to a certain radius. No matter how much the elephant desired to go beyond the limitations of the chain and the stake, it was bound and could not go any further. One day the elephant was unchained and was now free to move, but to the surprise of the observers, the elephant did not move past the area it had been restricted to by the chain.

The chain that bound the elephant's leg convinced the elephant that its world and boundaries were set by the chain. In essence, the chain on its leg had also successfully chained the elephant's mind.

Therefore, even though the physical bonds had been broken, failure to break the mental chains kept it confined. The only way to liberate the elephant would be to set it free mentally. How unfortunate that the elephant never got to read this book and be liberated.

Doesn't this story reflect our sad reality? Because though we have been liberated constitutionally and politically, we are still bound mentally. Only when the mental chains that have bound us for generations are broken will we truly break free from oppression and carve out a bright future that gives a full and authentic expression to who we truly are. We will then determine our destiny as a race – the self-determination that our ancestors dreamt about.

The dream of a liberated Black man will forever be impossible if we do not rid ourselves of the psychological shackles of slavery, colonialism and apartheid. Just as you cannot expect an athlete whose legs are chained to win a competition, we also cannot win if our minds are still chained and colonised. We cannot win in the race of the races if our minds are still chained, enslaved and colonised.

We need to break free from the shackles and fetters of the inferiority complex that made us believe the many lies, misconceptions and stereotypes dished out by the White man.

We need to redefine ourselves based on who we truly are and who we were created to be. We should stop looking at life and ourselves through the White man's lens which was intentionally designed to ensure that we remain slaves and cash cows forever.

For as long as we continue to define good and bad, acceptable and unacceptable, and wisdom and foolishness from the coloniser's perspective, we will forever remain chained. We will remain a cheap copy of the White man's identity instead of a genuine, divine and original identity.

Mnci struu, ke go botsa nnete! Ndiyakuxelela!

> *Where have you ever seen the majority weak and the minority strong? Only a mentally weak and helpless majority can allow this abnormal status quo to exist.*

Mind Invasion

The Italians, Americans, British and Hollanders invaded our land and eventually left. However, their invasion of our minds continues unabated to this day. Consequently, we have allowed the oppressors to commercialise their cultures, mannerisms, languages and tastes within our nations while our cultural tastes are trodden into the mud and die a slow and painful death.

Our minds have become so enslaved that we feel sophisticated and progressive when we dress and identify with fashion labels produced by White people.

Decades after Africa was decolonised, we still view style and fashion trends according to White people's dictates.

> *Just as you cannot expect an athlete whose legs are chained to win a competition, we also cannot win if our minds are still chained and colonised.*

We still derive worth and a sense of prestige from wearing the likes of Kurt Geiger, Tommy Hilfiger and Zara. We are so madly in love with convenience that we define ourselves by our former colonisers and oppressor's labels. What a coat of shame!

For as long as we remain guilty of such gullibility to colonial stereotypes, we are indeed still colonised. Where are the labels that should be making headlines in Africa? ***Labels by Africans for Africans.*** We should be ashamed of ourselves for not passionately promoting and advancing our own labels designed by our own African people.

Here we are in Africa, yet people sitting in New York, London, Beijing, Dubai and Paris control our tastes and minds. Inversely, our extremely talented indigenous designers go unnoticed and starve to death.

We have absolutely no business elevating colonial brands when we do nothing to promote and advance African brands.

Let us celebrate and brag about African designers. Let us empower and sow seeds of significance into them. The generations of our children and their children will reap the harvest of the seeds we sow today.

We are not using the power of our minds to break the chains that keep us loyal to foreign brands. The brand owners are chilling around the beaches of Europe, America and Asia, sipping on fine cognac and enjoying our money, while we stampede to acquire their brands. Yet they do not even plough a single cent back into the development of the African continent. All they ever do is rape us mercilessly.

> *The Italians, Americans, British and Hollanders invaded our land and eventually left. However, their invasion of our minds continues unabated to this day.*

This Must Change Black Man

We must remove the scales from our eyes if we wish to live to see the day of ultimate craze and passion about African labels.

We have what it takes to turn our cultural tastes into internationally renowned brands. Brands created by Africans who are full of black love, black pride, black dignity, black belief, black affirmation, black confidence, and black appreciation. We do not need to derive a sense of worth and value from colonial brands that do not express our historic, current and future identity.

We simply need to elevate and promote our own.

Viva Africa, Viva! Asijiki! Aluta Continua!

Please note that this does not mean the looting continues. This is targeted at our African political leaders who have looted our money and invested it in Switzerland. The looting stops here. Pun intended.

We should be confident enough to walk into boardrooms in our cultural attire developed and retailed by our own until all our children have pride in their roots and heritage.

We should proudly wear and aggressively promote made-in-African fashion brands. A few years from now, our children's children should be at the forefront of their own fashion industry and not be cash cows led to economic slaughterhouse to be chowed by the ravenous vampires to whom we are daily prey – the colonial designers.

We need the mental revolution to start now because we cannot hand down this deplorable state of mind and legacy to our forthcoming generations. It would be much better to die than pass this crap on to future generations.

Ons moet wakker word!
Phaphama muntu omnyama, siyadliwa la.
Ra jewa!
We are being ravaged here! This is a desperate wake-up call, Black man.

> *We should be confident enough to walk into boardrooms in our cultural attire developed and retailed by our own until all our children have pride in their roots and heritage.*

We Need a Shift from this Fruitless Mindset!

I once came across some information that revealed that the global multi-billion-dollar black hair industry is almost 100% owned by other races, even though Blacks are the target market. From extensions to relaxers, conditioners and others, Black people are non-existent in the entire value chain.

We are not benefitting in any way from this ludicrous and foolish process of trying to emulate whiteness.

The black hair industry thrives on other races identifying opportunities in the stupidity of Black people's *relentless attempts to flee their blackness*. They see Black people as cash cows whose foolishness will propel them into wealth.

If people can create multi-billion-dollar fortunes from your low self-esteem, self-hate, self-degradation, self-pity, and self-rejection, you must know that you need to strategically reposition yourself. Your position in the society is weak and pathetic!

The global fashion industry is another multi-billion-dollar industry propped up by Black people for the benefit of other races. Yet the fashion industry is one of the easiest industries to take advantage of; we should be capitalising on it and commercialising our tastes and styles.

We must start celebrating our own fashion designers. This is a market that Black people should start taking over by intentionally, deliberately, consciously and unashamedly producing, selling and buying designs by our imaginative brothers and sisters.

We already have fashion designers who have made a mark in our communities – the likes David Tlale, Ngugi Vere, Anita Mthimukhulu, Taetso Mashile (Scosh Leo), Wandile Zondo, Theo Baloyi (Bathu), Palesa Mokubung, Snoekie Mabena-Saleh (S.MAB Designs), Themba Makamo (ya Vaya),

Chenesai Mangoma (Chenesai Studio), Kgosi Nkosi, Sello Molekwa (Ayeye) and Mzukisi Mbane.

These are some of the black-owned fashion brands to obsess over and promote by spending money on them. These brands should not be just another option but our ***obsession***.

> *The black hair industry thrives on other races identifying opportunities in the stupidity of Black people's relentless attempts to flee their blackness.*

What Does This Say About Us?

Imagine with me for a moment, a black executive woman shows up for a board of directors meeting looking gracious, dignified and powerful; either in her full traditional *IsiZulu* attire (***isidwaba, ischolo namateki***) or in her Sepedi attire (***ntepa, hele, dipheta le di teki tse tshweu***). What do you see? I see pure and original African beauty.

Chances are high that if any shock or disapproval of this would come, it would be from fellow Black people. White people would probably consider it unprofessional and inappropriate, which is immaterial because we should not even care about what they think.

We need to be shameless and proud of our identity, culture and heritage and position ourselves to commercialise them to their fullest potential. We are a market significant enough to sustain our tastes and expressions of clothing as an industry.

As it is now, we are propelling European labels to dizzy heights at the expense of our people. Why can't we propel Black designers and brands to dizzy heights in Europe and the West?

Our cultural flair should not be restricted and reserved for Heritage Day or traditional weddings and functions. This thinking has long reached its expiry date. It must come to an immediate and screeching halt – *now-now, manje and janong*! The fact that this kind of thinking still prevails is evidence that we are not yet liberated in our minds.

We are still colonised! **Only that this time we are volunteering to be oppressed and colonised. We have become slaves by choice.**

Our preference to foreign brands is nothing short of voluntary enslavement and self-inflicted impoverishment.

> **We have absolutely no business elevating colonial brands when we do nothing to promote and advance African brands.**

Our Moral Obligation

We have a moral obligation to ensure that not only do we leave this world a better place for our offspring and generations to come, but that we also leave them in a better and more empowered state of mind.

We need to operate with a new mindset that says:

- *We, as Black people, have all it takes to set ourselves up for success.*
- *We do not need to use Whites as our crutches and points of reference.*
- *We can stand on our own and build a bright and illustrious future for ourselves.*

Can we claim that we would have lived purposeful and fulfilling lives if we do not empower our children to this effect?

We would be foolish to leave them with a rotten mindset that says true leadership and entrepreneurship are only found in White people's minds.

We should not allow that to happen!

We need to use the power of our minds to break every chain that paralyses our God-given talents and renders us incapable and incapacitated.

The chains that keep us seeking after White people's affirmation and approval must be broken.

Those chains must fall, and we are the only ones with the power to rid ourselves of them.

So, let us go ahead and break them. No more excuses! No more complaints! No more apportioning blame! The buck stops with us! Change starts with us!

"We are the ones we have been waiting for."

Barack Obama

We have a moral obligation to ensure that not only do we leave this world a better place for our offspring and generations to come, but that we also leave them in a better and more empowered state of mind.

7

BUSINESS UNUSUAL

"More than at any other time, the situation that confronts our nation and country and the tasks we have set ourselves demand that we inspire and organise all our people to act together as one, to do all the things that have to be done, understanding that in a very real sense, all of us, together, hold our own future in our hands. As we act together everywhere in our country, this we

must also understand that what we have to be about is – business unusual."

Thabo Mbeki

The South African economy is controlled and engineered by smart, shrewd, calculating and cunning brains. At the helm of industries are people who understand complex and intricate aspects of the economy. These minds set the tone of the economic climate. These shrewd brains position the white capitalist employers to stay ahead regardless of what happens at grassroots level.

The Harsh Reality: Economics 101

Whenever we talk about wealth redistribution, we come toe to toe with the economic Jacobs committed to ensuring that the scales are tipped in their favour as a race. In our foolishness, we confront these shrewd serpents with the attitude of Esau, the attitude of immediate gains.

A basic example is the annual industrial action that takes place in our country. Labour unions mobilise their members to press for increased wages and better working conditions. In all fairness they have the right to do so, but has this activity been effective?

A strike is a permanent and guaranteed fixture on our nation's events calendar. What are we striking for? Do we really get what we are striking for Black man? I mean, we have these strikes every year but are we really getting what we want? Are they effective or are we just aimlessly going through the motions? Or have we become so insane that we keep displaying the same stupidity that got us in this mess and expecting different outcomes?

Let us investigate this matter a little. When employees are not happy with their wages and working conditions they engage in collective bargaining with their employers hoping to improve their earnings and their working conditions. Refusing to be pushed over by economic weaklings, the employers refuse to grant their employees their requests. Frustrated by their reality, the employees down their tools and resort to issuing threats and physical violence, *"We will down our tools! We will shut down this plant! We will shut down this city and we will attack whoever decides go to work! "*

They go ahead and carry out their threats but come the following year, they are back on the streets holding placards and ***toyi-toying*** once more. The strike becomes another waste of energy, which yields no tangible results.

Therefore, we are active without being productive. It is like running on the treadmill – we are burning lots of energy but remaining in the same spot. The root of the problem is that we are vulnerable end consumers. Our behaviours empower the white monopoly capitalists to take advantage of our stupidity. This happens repeatedly.

In real terms our economic standing and our standard of living never changes for the better. The same employers who grant us the wage increases recoup them from us through price increases. We lose what we would have gained as soon as we would have gained it. We are once again brought back to square zero by these shrewd, calculative and cunning brains who we have made our *"lords"* because we love ease and convenience and do not want to build our own economy.

What Are You Saying, Black Man?

Black people are structurally disadvantaged. We are set up for continual defeat and demise because of our weak economic position. We break our backs to enrich the system of white monopoly capital, get paid peanuts, and spend those peanuts in a way that enriches the same system that is bent on keeping us down. This vicious cycle persists because we believe that we cannot live without white capitalists.

Remember, the Indians were at some stage worse off than we are. Yet today, they are far ahead of us because they came together, closed ranks, and decided to start empowering each other.

By adopting such an approach, we will ignite the long-awaited black economic revolution that our country needs. We do not need to *toyi-toyi* for this. We need to change how we think and do things.

Politicians will not do this for us, neither will they facilitate it. This is too radical for them. This is something that lies squarely on our shoulders as the average Black man on the street. Let us unite as Black people to effectively turn the economic tide in our favour.

Let us start in our communities and ignite the black economic revolution that our children will honour us for as they enjoy the fruit from the trees we would have planted.

We cannot just be thinking of ourselves. We should think ten to twenty generations ahead. **Amandla!**

> *We break our backs to enrich the system of white monopoly capital, get paid peanuts, and spend those peanuts in a way that enriches the same system that is bent on keeping us down.*

We Need to Start Making Changes

It has been more than twenty-seven years since the dawn of democracy, but Black South Africans are yet to set up a single supermarket chain that can take on the big boys in that space.

We still have not created one well-known chain store to play in the furniture space. We are still to come up with a retail clothing chain store that expresses our African tastes and culture.

We are still pushing and promoting our coloniser's brands like the *Louis Vuittons, Hermes', Pringle of Scotlands, Lacostes, Tommy Hilfigers,* and *Kurt Geigers* of this world. When would we proudly wear brands by a Zodwa Khoza, an Anita Mthimukulu, a Mzukisi Mbane, a Nthabiseng Ramadhivana, an Anisa Mpungwe, a Nkhensani

Nkosi, a Taetso Mashile, a David Tlale, or a Lerato Rammushi?

I mean quality cutting edge brands of excellence that express our expertise, culture and taste. When are we going to enjoy a bottle of fine whisky made by a Sipho Mkhize–Khabazela? I wish to live long enough to see the day when we would proudly, unapologetically and unashamedly celebrate and promote blackness over other cultures and tastes.

> *Let us unite as Black people to effectively turn the economic tide in our favour.*

Business Unusual

Our general concept of business needs to be redefined. We need to move towards a business model where the entire value chain benefits Blacks – from extraction of raw materials to agriculture, manufacturing, wholesaling, retailing, supplying, purchasing and exporting. This is where a chunk of wealth comes from.

The Chinese and Japanese realised this and learned the entire value chain process. While multinational corporations saw Asian countries as profitable business destinations, mainly because of the low costs of skilled labour, the Chinese and the Japanese refused to be mere employees. In the process of manufacturing for the Western and European masters, they committed to learning and understanding the entire process.

What you know as *fong kong*s emerged as Asian companies started mass productions of replicas of multinational companies. While South Africans mocked China for manufacturing *fong kongs*, the Chinese learning curve was becoming steeper. Today, they do not need those multinationals. They can produce products invented by multinationals themselves. From automobiles, cellphones, IT products, hi-tech equipment, clothing – the list goes on.

While at this, a stock take of the appliances in your home can reveal that most products you own are from Asia – the likes of Samsung, Huawei,

Sony, Panasonic and Hisense. As you travel to work, look out to spot a Toyota, Nissan, Mazda, Suzuki, Haval, Lexus, Hyundai and Kia. These are the products we brag about, manufactured in Asia, the same place we used to scorn for producing *fong kongs*.

For South Africa and Africa at large, there will be no shortcuts. This is the process and trajectory Black people must follow to achieve total economic emancipation.

Shosholoza!

What this means to us is, when we go to university, college, TVET, FET or whatever skills development programme we become a part of, the mentality we should carry is that we are in a learning process so we can be able to produce by and for ourselves. Please let it not just be to get a job and a salary at the end of the month. This kind of thinking must be fought and challenged on all fronts, especially in the home setting.

Parents, please drill this into the minds of your children – educate them to become producers and not just glorified, educated and qualified consumers. Teach them to be producers who will be responsible for the entire value chain.

To this, dedicate and commit your children and future generations. The revolution has begun!

> *Parents, please drill this into the minds of your children – educate them to become producers and not just glorified, educated and qualified consumers.*

8

WEALTH REDISTRIBUTION

"So, our people not only have to be re-educated to the importance of supporting black business, but the Black man himself has to be made aware of the importance of going into business.

And once you can create some employment in the community where you live, it will eliminate the necessity of you and me having to act ignorantly and disgracefully, boycotting and picketing someplace else trying to beg for a job.

Anytime you must rely upon your enemy for a job, you're in bad shape."

Malcolm X

By far and large, we agree that the wealth of our nation must be redistributed in favour of the birthright owner, the Black man. We may not agree on the methods, but we all agree on the principle. It must be done! ***Nomakanjani!***

However, in my view, we keep going round in circles in pursuit of this end. We erroneously believe that we can achieve wealth redistribution and real black economic empowerment by relying on politicians. This has proven to be total fallacy and failure. We do not appreciate that if we continue to rely on ready-made stew from the system as a solution for our weak economic position, we are digging ourselves into the bottomless pit of economic doom.

Until we accept that we can only attain stronger economic position by learning the fundamental principle of cooking our own stews and serving them to each other first, we will forever be trapped in the cycle of poverty and economic slavery. The starting point is circulating money amongst ourselves. Yes, amongst ourselves as Black people.

Unexplainable Facts

The population breakdown in South Africa, as per 2019 estimates by Statista is,

- 47.5 million Blacks,
- 4.4 million Whites,
- 5 million Coloureds and
- 1.45 million Indians/Asians.

Come to think of it, a whooping population of 47.5 million Black people and 5 million Coloureds are a ripe, juicy and sexy market for the 4.4 million Whites, and the 1.45 million Indians and Asians in our nation.

The majority of the 47.5 million Blacks are consumers and cheap labour for the White and Indian/Asian communities. They are unsuspecting, fat and gullible cash cows everyone is gunning for.

They feed everyone else while starving themselves to death.

What we do not realise is that these 47.5 million Black people are a dynamic and explosive nuclear economic power that propels and sustains the South African economy.

It is inconceivable that an economy resting on the shoulders of 47.5 million people, mostly benefits 5,9 million people. Considering that not all Whites, Indians and Asians are in business, we can conclude that 47.5 million people exist and work to enrich a tiny minority that is already filthy rich.

This picture cannot be justified in any way, shape or form. It is heart-breaking, painful and exponentially foolish for a population of 47.5 million Blacks and 5 million Coloureds to serve a tiny population of invaders.

I do not know about you, but this evokes a revolution in my heart and my mind.

After understanding that we collectively contribute to this picture through our thoughtless spending patterns, which leave us impoverished and economically vulnerable, I resolved in my heart of hearts to be extremely careful about how I spend every rand I earn. Lest this mess trickle down to my children, grandchildren, great-grandchildren and beyond.

Dear reader, considering such disturbing truth, what are you going to do about it?

How Do We Explain Our Anomalies?

Let's look at the following anomalies maybe you can tell me how we could explain this to our children:

- *How do we explain the anomaly that Black people, being the largest consumers of bread, do not own a competitive brand of bread?*
- *How do we explain the anomaly that maize meal (also known as mealie meal), the staple food of Black people of Mzansi, is produced by white companies? White people do not consume pap as their staple food, Blacks do. But here we are, looking to the minority Whites to spoon-feed us a product they stole from us. No! No! No!*
- *Where are the Black people who will see the glaring opportunity to start bakeries that supply bread to our townships?*

- *Where are the Black people who will take the opportunity to produce mealie meal and supply it to their communities?*
- *A whooping market of 47.5 million customers! Where are the Black people who will take advantage of this blatant opportunity?*
- *How do we explain this madness? About 47.5 million Black people rely on 4.4 million Whites and 1.45 million Indians and Asians to feed, clothe, educate, house, employ, and produce most of what Black people consume?*
- *How do we explain 47.5 million people who cannot create a clothing industry that promotes their culture, tastes and preferences?*

White Monopoly Capitalists

Is it not amazing how Black people complain about white monopoly capitalists? In our view, white capitalism is the chief source of our problems, poverty and frustrations.

In that connection, let us take a step back and ask ourselves, what makes white monopoly capitalists so strong and seemingly invincible? Don't look too far for the answer, it is right under your nose. The black consumer population created white monopoly capitalists and continues to sustain them to this day.

Simple Bread and Pap

I will limit my reference to the issue of bread and maize meal. How do we explain the dominant brands of mealie meal, which are very few and white-owned, supplying the entire Black population of South Africa? As stated earlier, White people do not consume mealie meal as a staple, Black people do.

Come to think of it, mealie meal is an invention of Black people, which White people stole and are now its monopoly producers.

Simply put, we created white monopolies of mealie meal. Now hear me, we should start thinking of creating black monopolistic producers of mealie meal. This will be the beginning of the end of our self-sabotage.

There is absolutely no need for 47.5 million people to depend on a few white monopoly companies to produce and distribute mealie meal. Black people all over South Africa should position themselves to produce maize meal and supply it to their townships. For example, in the township of Soweto there should be between four to six black-owned millers that supply its population. This would be real economic empowerment. Extrapolate this concept across the many townships in our country; we could be looking at hundreds of black businesses who produce mealie meal, becoming financially empowered in tandem.

For effective redistribution of wealth, the powerful black majority should create and support decentralisation of monopolies.

It is self-defeating to hope that wealth will be redistributed while we continuously support white monopolies.

The same argument holds for bread. Every township can have two or three bakeries that produce and supply bread to the community. In that way, we create more black businesses that will employ more Black people.

Strategically and intentionally, this should be the way forward regarding all the various industries until the Black man achieves total economic dominance and financial liberation.

The only way that wealth will be redistributed is by moving away from supporting and sustaining white monopoly businesses while we begin our own business endeavours which we have a lifetime of generations to grow and establish. A centralised economy where only a few white minorities benefit from the efforts of a majority is tantamount to self-assassination.

Additionally, other industries such as clothing, agriculture and retail must be decentralised in favour of emerging black businesses.

Position yourself, Black man.

B4 Loading ...

As alluded to in previous chapters, Black people are powerful yet hopelessly dependent because they are mentally enslaved. We are heavily dependent on the ruthless and greedy minority who do not spare a punch in exploiting our blatant foolishness, ignorance and snoring sleepiness.

Black man, remember that you must run faster or forever remain behind.

You are literally on your own.

Watch out, you are in serious trouble.

> *Black people are powerful yet hopelessly dependent because they are mentally enslaved.*

The Tide Must Turn

Black man, it is relatively easy to venture into the few industries I mentioned above. Let us take, own and control them for our benefit for a start.

When we defeated apartheid, we liberated ourselves politically. Now we must liberate ourselves economically. We must achieve wealth redistribution as a matter of urgency; and it begins with emancipating ourselves from the mental enslavement that keeps us believing that we need these ruthless minorities. We don't need them!

The apartheid system was deliberately designed to make us mental and economic slaves who are oblivious to their potential, power and God-given abilities.

It is clear that even though we are structurally liberated, we remain mentally and economically oppressed and we further oppress ourselves by embracing whatever comes our way from ruthless capitalist minorities.

There is something drastically wrong with this current status quo. We can go on and on expanding on this, twisting and turning it, but whichever way you look at it, it is wrong and deplorable.

We need to break these chains off. We need to break this cycle of mental enslavement and economic dependency.

We must refuse to find ourselves in the same situation ten, twenty, thirty, fifty and a hundred years from now.

Break those chains, my Black brother and sister! Break those chains loose and be the captain of your destiny! Imagine Tasha Cobbs singing her famous song, *"Break Every Chain"* and see those mental chains breaking.

Come on somebody, say *"Amen."* Shout, *"Amen"* once again.

We Can Start Here and Now

I reiterate, the most effective way to initiate an economic liberation movement is by practising the wisdom of circulating money amongst ourselves.

This revolution will most definitely empower us and thrust us into the mainstream of the economy of our country.

Truth be told, Whites need Blacks much more than Blacks need them.

A Blow Below the Belt

This is another post I came across on social media. Dee Lee – a qualified accountant in the USA – has distanced herself from this article. This, therefore, suggests that there must be another person by the same name who wrote this, or the author used a fake name to conceal their identity.

Regardless of the author's identity, what remains is that somebody, who may have been a Black or White man, wrote this.

I know that some of you may have come across this post before but let us go through it together again.

This time, let us do so with a sober mind coupled with a serious, ruthless and robust introspection.

> **THEY ARE STILL OUR SLAVES**
>
> *We can continue to reap profits from the blacks without the effort of physical slavery. Look at the current methods of containment that they use on themselves:* **IGNORANCE, GREED** *and* **SELFISHNESS.**
>
> *Their* **IGNORANCE** *is the primary weapon of containment. A great man once said,* **'The best way to hide something from Black people is to put it in a book, because you can be sure they will not read it.'**
>
> *We now live in the Information Age. They have gained the opportunity to read any book on any subject through the efforts of their fight for freedom, yet they refuse to read.* **(Is this still going to be the case with this book?)**
>
> *There are numerous books readily available at Borders, Barnes & Noble, and Amazon.com, not to mention their black bookstores that provide solid*

blueprints to reach economic equality (which should have been their fight all along), but few read consistently, if at all....

GREED *is another powerful weapon of containment. Blacks, since the abolition of slavery, have had large amounts of money at their disposal.*

Last year they spent 10 billion dollars during Christmas, out of their 450 billion dollars in total yearly income (2.22%).

Any of us can use them as our target market, for any business venture we care to dream up, no matter how outlandish, they will buy into it.

Being primarily a consumer people, they function totally by greed. They continually want more, with little thought for saving or investing.

They would rather buy some new sneakers than invest in starting a business. Some even neglect their children to have the latest Tommy or FUBU and they still think that having a Mercedes and a big house gives them 'Status' or that they have achieved their Dream.

They are fools!

The vast majority of their people are still in poverty because their greed holds them back from collectively making better communities.

With the help of B.E.T (Black Entertainment Television) and the rest of their black media that often broadcasts destructive images into their own homes, we will continue to see huge profits like those of Tommy and Nike. (Tommy Hilfiger has even jeered them, saying he doesn't want their money and look at how the fools spend more with him than ever before!).

They'll continue to show off to each other, while we build solid communities with the profits from the businesses that we market to them. OUCH!

SELFISHNESS, ingrained in their minds through slavery, is one of the major ways we can continue to contain them. One of their own, W. E.B Dubois said that there was an innate division in their culture. A 'Talented Tenth' he called it. He was correct in his deduction that there are segments of their culture that have achieved some 'form' of success.

However, that segment missed the fullness of his work. They didn't read that the 'Talented Tenth' was then responsible to aid The Non-Talented Ninety Percent in achieving a better life. Instead, that segment has created another class, a Buppie class that looks down on their people or aids them in a condescending manner.

They will never achieve what we have... Their selfishness does not allow them to be able to work together on any project or endeavour of substance.

When they do get together, their selfishness lets their egos get in the way of their goal. Their so-called help organizations seem to only want to promote their name without making any real change in their community.

They are content to sit in conferences and hold conventions in our hotels and talk about what they will do, while they award plaques to the best speakers, not to the best doers.

> *Is there no end to their foolishness? They steadfastly refuse to see that Together, Each Achieves More (TEAM).*
>
> *They do not understand that they are no better than each other because of what they own, as a matter of fact, most of those Buppies are but one or two pay checks away from poverty. All of which is under the control of our pens in our offices and our rooms.*
>
> *Yes, we will continue to contain them as long as they refuse to read, continue to buy anything they want, and keep thinking they are 'helping' their communities by paying dues to organizations that do little other than hold lavish conventions in our hotels.*
>
> *By the way, don't worry about any of them reading this letter, remember,* **'THEY DON'T READ!!!!**

Can I ask a favour from all Black people? Let us not concern ourselves with whether it was a Black or White person who wrote this. Let us, with a brutal, ruthless and no holds barred honesty, accept that this is the truth about us!

Let us take some time to break down this bitter truth and intentionally rub it into our skins, as painful as it may be.

Let us not even try to defend ourselves from these hard facts. We are taking this bull by its horns to deal with it.

Let the rumble begin, we are indeed as stated:

- *Not readers. Instead of investing in books, we would rather buy their fashion labels to show off to each other.*

We are currently living under a shameful scourge in most of our townships. There are no bookshops and/or community libraries. At most, communities lucky enough to have libraries meet empty shelves with each visit. Yet many pubs, taverns and shebeens in our communities are prospering.

Even the shopping malls that are mushrooming in our townships have no bookshops at all. You will find many liquor stores and fashion outlets. Bookshops *dololo!*

Selah! Reflect upon this. Readers are leaders!

- *Profuse consumers who are mostly ready to buy what we do not need just to be seen by others.*

Edward Norton defined our behaviour well when he said, *"We buy things we don't need, with money we don't have, to impress people we don't like."*

We buy things to impress people who do not like us. As a result, we remain poor, dependent and vulnerable, leaving nothing behind for our children and grandchildren.

- *Easy targets. Any of them can use us as their target market, for any business venture they care to dream up, no matter how outlandish, we will buy into it. We are gullible consumers!*

When somebody who has become extremely wealthy from your foolishness goes to the extent of mocking you, be sure they believe and think you are irreversibly stupid.

They believe they can continue grabbing you by the balls and squeezing them hard and you will forever suffer in silence like a sheep being slaughtered.

Think and think hard about this, Black man.

This is sad!

We are perceived as easy targets. Most businesses that make money from our communities belong to people of other races.

Imagine how they encourage each other to start businesses in our communities. They probably say to each other, *"Let us go after those easy targets, because our victory is certain."*

Lately, the Pakistanis have realised this painful reality about us.

- *The vast majority of our people are still in poverty because our greed holds us back from collectively building better communities.*

Black man, listen to me carefully. Please be comfortable, breathe in, breathe out, and relax.

I hope you are ready to face this harsh reality.

The truth is this is how most White people perceive Black people. Finish and *Klaar!* They think we are greedy, profuse consumers, ignorant non-readers and easy targets.

There is a *Sepedi* phrase that says, **"Botlaela gabo alafege, bophala ke bogafi!"** Meaning, you have a better chance of curing madness than foolishness.

What are we going to do?

> *The apartheid system was deliberately designed to make us mental and economic slaves who are oblivious to their potential, power and God-given abilities.*

Never Again

In addition to the above, let us also consider the statements below. The writer is unknown but some have suggested it might have been Steve Biko. At this point it is immaterial who the author is; the message is real, clear and painful.

These postulations about our race should trigger robust and merciless conversations within the Black nation.

We should not allow ourselves off the hook until we are completely liberated and can look at this kind of writings, laugh aloud and say: *"It used to be true about us but not anymore."*

CHARACTERISTICS OF A DEFEATED RACE

- *A race that brags about the cars that they drive, that are manufactured by companies owned by another race.*
- *A race that brags about their houses that are financed by financial institutions owned by another race.*
- *A race that takes their kids to school to be taught by another race.*
- *A race that will celebrate their wedding in the style of another race.*
- *A race that has fully adopted the language of another race.*
- *A race that will hate each other while defending another race.*
- *A race that will get excited to work for another race.*
- *A race that the only freedom it has is the freedom to vote and not economic freedom.*

> - *A race that will kill each other just to have a political position and be in the office and not be in power.*
> - *A defeated race is that race that is in the majority, but its survival relies on the minority race.*
>
> *Are we a defeated race?*

Ouch! Yet another blow below the belt.
Did you feel it like I did?
It never rains, it pours!

We Are the Restless Ones

Sad as the perceptions held about us may be, I consider our generation of indigenous Africans a blessed one.

- *We are the determined ones ready to take the bull by its horns and confront the things we used to turn a blind eye on!*
- *We are the liberated generation that will not be defined or mastered by anyone!*
- *We are the defiant and rebellious ones who will not bow down to the image of black inferiority and white supremacy!*

- We are the restless ones who will break the yoke from our necks and walk in economic, political, cultural, ideological and mental freedom!
- We are the controversial misfits who will challenge the status quo of mediocrity and change the narrative of our race!
- We are the history makers and the world changers our race has been wishing for!
- We are the ones we have been waiting for!
- We are the ones who will change our destiny.
- We are the selfless ones who embrace economic revolution as a non-negotiable and absolute necessity!

Until total economic dominance is achieved by the Black man and the wealth of the country is redistributed in accordance with the population demographics of the nation, we will not relent!

Asijiki!

Aluta Continua!

Our mantra is, *"Total Economic Liberation or Death!"*

B4 Loading...

Our Resolution

Let us resolve to never ignore the critical issues that affect the future of our race. For the sake of our children, grandchildren, great-grandchildren and a thousand generations to come, we will roll up our sleeves, put on our work suits, and soldier on to secure genuine freedom for the Black man.

As the biblical Nehemiah took up the challenge to rebuild the walls of Jerusalem, we are taking it upon ourselves, as a generation, the mammoth task of rebuilding the fallen walls of our race, communities, dignity and pride.

Izwe Lethu!

Freedom is Coming!

A hundred years ago, countries like China, Japan, and South Korea were all poor rural countries. Fast-forward a hundred years later, these countries are now economic powerhouses to be reckoned with.

China and Japan have even evolved into leading global economies only surpassed by the United States. They have even overtaken Europe.

Who would have imagined the possibility of that a hundred years ago?

Sibiya Generations

My grandfather, Ben Ndukwana Sibiya, was born in 1890 and my first-born son, Mandlenkosi Mamela Sibiya, was born in 1990. Between my grandfather and my son is a period of a hundred years. Therefore, a hundred is not as much a long time as we may think.

A hundred years can easily represent four generations: the generations of my grandfather, my father, mine and my son's.

If we can completely turn the current status quo around in four generations, we would have done our future generations a great service. Some of you might live long enough to enter our Promised Land. However, the satisfaction is in knowing that our offspring will.

Hence, we must start now! We must be willing to pay whatever price is required!

The Promised Land:

Our Hundred Years from Now

If you and I were to rise from the grave a hundred years from now, I am confident beyond a shadow of doubt that the following is what you will see:

- *You will see the full restoration of our birthright as a people.*
- *You will see the undeniable fruit of this black cultural and economic revolution – the one we are about to start.*
- *You will see communities where:*
  - *Our race and its diverse cultures are honoured and celebrated.*
  - *Our languages are proudly spoken.*
  - *Our people live in peace and harmony.*
  - *Our people circulate money amongst themselves.*
  - *Our institutions deliver exceptional service to our people. From schools to hospitals, businesses, government departments, etc.*
  - *Our people are producers and innovators and not just consumers and spectators.*

- *Our people are without generational debt and are passing on generational wealth to their posterity.*

- *You will see an advanced and thriving black economy.*
- *You will see Black people in the driving seat of the economy.*
- *You will see Black people controlling most of the country's wealth.*
- *You will see Black people really and truly proud to be black!*

"When you continue to blame someone, you give up the power to change"

Dr David Molapo

If you still have time today, please do not finish this book. Put it down, find yourself a place where you can be alone and come up with a personal plan of action regarding how you will contribute and participate in this imminent community-driven revolution.

Change for our race begins with us. *"We are the ones our ancestors have been waiting for."*

9

YES, WE CAN!

"This is our moment...while we breathe, we hope. And where we are met with cynicism and doubts and those who tell us that we can't, we will respond with that timeless creed that sums up the spirit of a people: Yes, we can."

Barack Obama

A united minority of 5,85 million (Whites and Indians) are stronger and more effective than a divided majority of 52,5 million (Blacks and Coloureds). *Selah!*

The history of Black people in South Africa shows that power and strength do not lie in numbers but in unity.

Our challenge as Black people is the lack of unity and collaboration skills.

A Story to Ponder

Once upon a time before any civilisation ever existed, during a time when the whole earth spoke one language, a group of people set out to build a city with a tower that reached to the heavens. These ancient people understood each other and could communicate on a stance of complete unity. They were of one mind.

A project of this magnitude had never been attempted before. It was as unprecedented as JF Kennedy's dream to send a man to the moon and back to earth. This was a big, hairy and audacious vision.

However, the unity of the people certainly brought this audacious vision within reach.

Their unity made them a well-oiled operation and a force to reckon with.

Their extremely bold vision gained traction because there were no obstacles caused by division.

United, they shared ideas, insights, expertise, influence, opportunities, experiences and perspectives on how they would achieve the mammoth task before them.

Their hard resolve, unwavering commitment and fiery passion set their meetings, operations and conversations so ablaze that the Lord God took notice and acknowledged that their unity set them on course to attain the result they were after.

Remember the phrase, *"United we stand, divided we fall"*? It is true of the Black race as it is of any other race.

When we unite, we exponentially multiply our power. New possibilities spring up, impossibilities fade into oblivion, limitations melt like wax before a fire, when Black people come together behind a singular vision and agenda.

Remember how the system of apartheid was brought down in 1994? It came about because of unity.

Yes, that almost impossible to overcome system of apartheid came down when we united and sang *Shosholoza, Thula Sizwe* and *Freedom is Coming Tomorrow*. We chipped away at the evil beast of apartheid.

The story above is well articulated in Genesis 11 v 4 – 9. Below is a brief account of it.

[4] "Then they said, "Come, let us build ourselves a city, with a tower that reaches to the heavens, so that we may make a name for ourselves; otherwise, we will be scattered over the face of the whole earth."

[5] But the Lord came down to see the city and the tower the people were building.

[6] The Lord said, "If as one people speaking the same language, they have begun to do this, then nothing they plan to do will be impossible for them.

[7] Come, let us go down and confuse their language so they will not understand each other."

[8] So the Lord scattered them from there over all the earth, and they stopped building the city.

[9] That is why it was called Babel---because there the Lord confused the language of the whole world. From there the Lord scattered them over the face of the whole earth."

We read in Genesis 11 of a people Bible scholars believe were Black people. Their resolve was to unite to build a city, with a tower that reaches to the heavens, so that they can make a name for themselves and not be scattered over the face of the earth.

These people were so determined that they even drew the attention of God, who decided they needed to be checked out.

When God saw their unity and determination, He spoke the following words: *"If as one people speaking the same language they have begun to do this, then nothing they plan to do will be impossible for them"*.

I want you to note that God dismantled their plan because they were extremely arrogant. Their main reason to pull off this project was to spite God.

The story could probably have turned out differently had they acknowledged God in their endeavour and decided to build the tower to the Glory of God.

I would like us to draw some principles out of this story.

If, We, As One People

Unity in purpose and direction is extremely crucial if Black people are to achieve anything of significance.

If this is something that we must learn from scratch, so be it. It is generally accepted that Black people do not do very well when it comes to unity.

We are a divided people; thus, a potential danger to ourselves. May God above and our common ancestry unite us towards a common vision as a race.

How Disturbing This Is

I once came across a video clip where a white supremacist said the following:

"We as Whites do not have to do anything to achieve the destruction of Black people, they are well capable of doing it all by themselves, all we need to do is to give them guns, drugs and a lot of alcohol. They will self-destruct". Selah!

Please find a few people you can discuss this statement with and interrogate it.

We must do all that is in our power to prove this man wrong. We may still have a long way to go to achieve this, but we owe it to ourselves to prove assertions like this wrong.

May God give us strength to do so!

IN REFLECTION

I would like us to reflect on the biblical reference that opened this book. Esau sold his birthright for the convenience of ready-made stew. This stupidity resulted in him serving instead of being served.

The final words spoken by Isaac to Esau are crucial. I would like us to reflect on them.

"But when you grow restless, you will throw his yoke from off your neck."

Let us recap on what this yoke is:

"I have made him lord over you and have made all his relatives his servants, and I have sustained him with grain and new wine."

So, even though Esau sold his birthright and was relegated to serve Jacob, he would eventually break that yoke from off his neck, if he would become restless enough to do something about it.

He would wake up and realise that he had the power to reverse the consequences of his stupidity. He would wake up to take his rightful leadership position – the one in which he is to be served and not serve others; where he is the head again and not the tail; and where he is in control of his destiny.

For the reasons of liberating and empowering Black people and for restoring the Black nation to its rightful place of honour and dignity, I wrote this book. I also engage in conversations around these issues all the time.

I want to agitate the Black nation out of its false sense of comfort and shake it into a restless disposition.

We cannot allow the mental and economic oppression by a minority to prevail over the majority.

We should get out of this situation and empower our children to this sole end – *breaking the oppressor's yoke from our necks.*

Rise Black Man

Black man rise and take your rightful position!

Africa is your home. It is rich in minerals of gold, silver, diamonds, platinum and many more given to you by your Creator and stolen from you by the oppressor.

You have no business being poor and depending on a White man for economic leadership and sustenance.

God had your best interest at heart when he placed you in Africa.

As Bob Marley sang, "... *emancipate yourselves from mental slavery ... none but ourselves can free our minds ...*". No one can do it for you. Rise and take responsibility for your destiny!

I imagine God saying to the Black man:

- *You were never destined to be poor and desolate. You were never destined to be controlled by people who found you in a home I have provided for you. Rise and take your rightful place!*

- *You were never destined to put the interests of others above your own. Rise and take your rightful place!*
- *You were never destined to promote the languages of your oppressor above your own. Your African language is a gift that I have given you. You must treasure it, protect it and love it. Rise and take your rightful place!*
- *You were never destined to be a cheap copy of someone else's image. I gave you a distinct culture and identity which must never be overshadowed by anyone. You must give full expression to your culture and identity even in this era of advancement and technology. Rise and take your rightful place!*
- *You were never destined to show more interest in music that does not give full expression of who you are and where you come from. I am surprised that almost 90% of the music you play on your local radio stations is foreign music and yet you have an avalanche of talented local artists who go unnoticed and hungry. When are you going to recognise, appreciate and promote local black talent? Stop acting like a fool, Black man. Rise and take your rightful place!*

Now that we heard the call from our Creator to go back to whom He created us to be, to return to the originality He envisaged when He designed us to be different but not inferior, the ball is in our court.

We have the masses and knowledge necessary to break the chains of colonialism and oppression that have kept us subjugated for generations. However, knowledge and numbers are inadequate. Passion will nudge us into action.

The time to begin the journey to recovery and reclaim our rightful place in the race of races has come.

- *We will make the sacrifices required for the sake of future generations.*
- *We will make the sacrifices required for the sake of future generations.*
- *We will make the sacrifices required for the sake of future generations.*
- *We will make the sacrifices required for the sake of future generations.*
- *We will make the sacrifices required for the sake of future generations.*

Though we might not live long enough to realise the fruits of the seeds we are planting, we are inspired that our descendants will enjoy the fruits of our toil.

There is no better time to start than now.

Ke nako. Isikhathi sesifikile. Nkari wu fikile!

Our time is now!

It is do or die, Black man!

It is now or never!

ACKNOWLEDGEMENTS

To the following people who have contributed immensely to my life, I salute and honour you for believing in me while I was struggling to believe in myself:

My spiritual father, Archbishop Dr Abraham Thamsanqa Sibiya,

My brothers, Donald Sibiya, Mthokozisi Andrew Sibiya, Pastor Vusi Sibiya, and my younger sisters, Pastor Sibongile Sibiya, Siphelele Sibiya and Dr Simangele Ntuli together with her husband Sam Ntuli.

The Pastors I serve with, and the congregation that I lead, at Christ-Centred Chapel of Grace,

To Sello Molekwa, your partnership in this project was amazing and invaluable.

To my Pastor Edwin Ngoni Tawengwa, thanks for helping with the English language and your leadership of this project. Your proficiency with the language shows that the white man effectively colonised you. You speak his language better than yours. *Ndinotenda Zvikuru!*

To my editor Emelia Mosima, thank you very much for your invaluable input and raising the standard of editorial excellence of this manuscript.

To Dr Trevor Majoro, thank you for working with me throughout this project. *Hola bra yami!*

To my proofreader Dr Lizzy Peega for your invaluable contribution, insight and critique of this work.

I am not ashamed to admit that all these people have helped me to stretch and grow into the person I am today.

My line of thinking in this book has been shaped and influenced greatly by the questions that I have been carrying from my youth, my observations as I was travelling through this journey of life, the sermons of my friend and Pastor of Friendship West Baptist Church, Dr Frederick

Douglas Haynes, and the writings of Chika Onyeani, author of *Capitalist Nigger*.

Not forgetting the inspiring legacies left by the founding fathers of Africa's liberation. Thank you for passing the baton.

I would also like to honour the legacies of Dr Martin Luther King Jnr, and Malcolm X. These legends have achieved immortality.

To my friend in law, Cheryl Valerie Chigodora, thank you for your support.

Final note: Inspired people, inspire people. If this book has inspired you, please inspire others with it.

It is my prayer that you be the ambassador of the message of this book and help spread the word widely. Never rest till every Black person has read this book.

Amandla!!!!! Viva Africa Viva!!!!! Rise Black Man Rise!!!!

ABOUT THE AUTHOR

Black Self-Love Advocate Sakhile Sibiya is a Pastor, community builder, entrepreneur, thought leader and diversity consultant whose driving passion is to change the black man's perspective of self, his fellow black men, and the rest of the human race.

For the past 25 years he has worked tirelessly to improve the prospects of his community Soshanguve and Black people at large through a host of empowerment programs targeted mainly at men, youth, entrepreneurs and leaders.

Sakhile is also the Founder of Batho Bathso Bakopane Bathekgana (B4), a grassroots movement that is calling Black people back to self-love and to advancing Black interests.

CONNECT WITH US

For enquiries, bookings, orders, and information regarding our events and movement, please kindly subscribe, like, follow and contact us on these platforms.

 @sakhilewabantu

 @sakhilewabantu

 facebook.com/sakhilewabantu1

 Sakhile waBantu

🌐 www.sakhilesibiya.com

✉ info@sakhilesibiya.co.za

www.ingramcontent.com/pod-product-compliance
Lightning Source LLC
Chambersburg PA
CBHW060108170426
43198CB00010B/821